PERSONAL SAFETY FOR SCHOOLS

This book, published in the 10th Anniversary of The Suzy Lamplugh Trust, is the third in a series commissioned by the Trust.

Related titles:

Personal Safety for Social Workers
Personal Safety for Health Care Workers

Personal Safety
for
Schools

Diana Lamplugh
Barbara Pagan

arena

Published by
Arena
Ashgate Publishing Limited
Gower House
Croft Road
Aldershot
Hants GU11 3HR
England

Ashgate Publishing Company
Old Post Road
Brookfield
Vermont 05036
USA

British Library Cataloguing in Publication Data

Lamplugh, Diana
  Personal safety for schools
  1. School employees – Assaults against – Great Britain –
  Prevention 2. Self-defence 3. Violence in the workplace
  I. Title II. Pagan, Barbara
  362.8'8'02437

Library of Congress Catalog Card Number: 96-86202

ISBN 1 85742 194 9

Typeset in Palatino by Raven Typesetters, Chester
Printed In Great Britain by Hartnolls Ltd, Bodmin

Contents

Preface

This book, commissioned by The Suzy Lamplugh Trust, the national charity for personal safety, appears in a period of great concern for the safety of those who work in education. Tragically, 1995 and 1996 will be remembered as years when pupils were killed by intruders into their schools, and a head-master was killed at the school gate, trying to defend one of his pupils.

Even before these horrifying crimes took place, it had been clear for some time that violence and aggression were on the increase, and that no work-place was immune. Ten years after Suzy Lamplugh disappeared in the course of her work as an estate agent negotiator in what appeared, in 1986, to be an unusual crime, we now know that it would be foolish for employees – particularly those who deal with people on a daily basis – to believe that they are unlikely ever to meet with violence – more foolish still, to assume that they would be able to cope in all circumstances.

Recent membership surveys by teacher unions all point to the fact that assaults on teachers are on the increase, that many teachers suffer daily abuse and, on occasion, threats from pupils and parents. In 20 per cent of schools, pupils themselves have also been assaulted by non-members of the school or adults connected with the school.[1]

Other research also underlines what has become a worrying situation for society in general, and for schools and colleges in particular. For instance, the University of Exeter's research for the Channel 4 programme *Dispatches* in 1996, revealed, incredibly, that the UK has a child population in which a quarter of 11-year-olds and a third of 16-year-olds claim to be carrying weapons, some even guns.[2] These grim findings match those of a recent Trust survey.

Written for those who work in education, this book is the third in a series – the first two having been written for social workers and for workers in health disciplines. All three professions face aggression, and sometimes violence, from those individuals for whom they have a duty of care. In addition, those who teach, and those who support them, have to meet with their 'clients' all day and every day, exercising a role which may well be viewed by pupils as one of enforcement, rather than caring. This factor in itself adds tremendously to the stresses and strains of this particular workplace.

This book is in part written for those whose responsibility it is to ensure the security of education establishments, namely governing bodies. When considering the personal safety of employees, governors, with senior management, are required to make the premises as secure as the layout and design of the workplace will allow, not only for the safety of staff, but also to prevent theft, arson and vandalism. In addition, those responsible for security in educational establishments will need to adopt an integrated approach to the wider question of personal safety through the training of staff in the management of aggression, and, in schools and colleges, through appropriate curricular provision for pupils and students

Clearly, this book has, in the main, teachers in mind, but it does not only consider the problems of those who work in schools and colleges. Where appropriate, it also considers safety procedures for those in other education-related work. For instance those who may have to travel a great deal in the course of their work, such as advisers, inspectors, NVQ assessors and verifiers, and other outreach workers, or who have to negotiate with pupils and their parents in the family home, as do education welfare officers.

It should be noted in passing that although this book is not about the discipline of pupils, it is nevertheless arguable that those skills which support personal safety, communication, negotiation and assertiveness also relate to the successful management of children.

Part 1 looks at violence in the context of the law, the workplace and the community.

Part 2 then goes on to examine the responsibilities of governors and managers, and suggests ways of undertaking risk assessment and arriving at a school safety policy.

Part 3 looks at ways of reducing the risks in the workplace, and touches upon the responsibilities of employees themselves.

Part 4 defines skills for personal safety.

Part 5 is for professional trainers in personal safety, who may be called upon to train staff in educational establishments, and who may not themselves have worked in education.

We should be remiss if we did not acknowledge how much this book has grown in the making. It has benefited enormously from the excellent advice of many of the members of the DfEE Working Group on School Security set up following the tragic death of headteacher Philip Lawrence, and whose report, *School Security: The Report of the Working Group*, was published by the DfEE in May 1996.[3] Our grateful thanks are due to all those of the Working Group who read the manuscript while this was still at an early stage, and who gave us the benefit of their experience, insight and judgement.

We note with interest that as well as urging schools, among other things, to continue to review their security, particularly control of access, the Working Group points to the need for governors to receive more support to help them fulfil their security responsibilities, and for teachers, support staff and governors to be given appropriate training.

Finally, our thanks are also due to Sue Littman, who so patiently typed this manuscript, Anne Strahan for checking all the references, and Charlotte Batchelor for undertaking the proofreading.

No doubt, the debate and the discussions about school security and the safety of those who work in education will continue. It is our hope that this book will assist that debate.

References

1   Association of Teachers and Lecturers, Manchester Branch (1996), *Survey of Assaults on Teachers in Manchester City Schools*, press release.
2   Balding, J. et al. (1996), *Cash and Carry*, Schools Health and Education Unit, Exeter University.
3   Department for Education and Employment (1996), *School Security: Report of the Working Group*, London: DfEE.

Acknowledgements

The authors are grateful to the following members of the DfEE Working Group on School Security:

John Andrews – Professional Association for Teachers
Vivian Anthony – Headmasters' and Headmistresses' Conference/Girls' Schools Association
Roy Atkinson – Association of County Councils
John Bangs – National Union of Teachers
Gavin Bye – Health and Safety Executive
Gwenlian Evans – Association of Teachers and Lecturers
Simon Goulden – Agency for Jewish Education
David Lankshear – Church of England Board of Education
Alan Parker – Association of Metropolitan Authorities
Rob Smith – Department for Education and Employment, Chairman of the DfEE Working Group
John Sutton – Secondary Heads Association
Stephen Williams – Department for Education and Employment, Secretary of the DfEE Working Group

The authors are also grateful to the following for their help and support:

Mrs Castle – Headmistress, Cheltenham Ladies College
Chief Inspector Bill Croft – Home Office Crime Prevention College (part of the Home Office Crime Prevention Agency)
Dr Groves – Senior Admissions Officer, Marlborough College
Mrs Hylson-Smith – Headmistress, Westonbirt School
Mrs Padfield – Senior Mistress, Dean Close School

Personal safety audit

Do you need this book?

Dealing with aggression can be an almost daily routine for some who work in education. In addition, there may be certain site-related risks which you take every day without realizing it. Review your situation from time to time, with the following checks.

Concerning your place of work

- Are there areas where you feel uneasy (e.g. poorly-lit entrances, corridors or walkways; car parks, classrooms or offices away from the main block)?
- Are there main entrances to the site which are open at all times? If so, who has these within their line of vision?
- Are you ever alone at work (e.g. when working early or late)?
- Are there other times of day when you feel particularly vulnerable? What can you do to help yourself to feel safer?
- If returning home after dark, have you considered possible risks (e.g. where you parked the car, how you will reach public transport)?
- Has any risk assessment been carried out with regard to your place of work?
- Is there provision for you to keep your personal possessions safe and out of sight?

Dealing with aggression

- Can you recognize facial expressions or hand, head and body movements which give early warning of agitation or aggression? Have you considered what responses are appropriate and might reduce the level of aggression?

- If a visitor to the site is aggressive, do you know what to do? Do you have ways of summoning assistance, if necessary?
- If you work with a group which has potentially aggressive or threatening individuals in it, do you have ways of summoning assistance, as well as an escape route?
- Is there a system for reporting incidents of aggressive behaviour, or raising matters concerning perceived risks? Are all staff aware of the system? Are these incidents taken seriously by those to whom they are reported?
- Are there certain individuals who make you feel uncomfortable or uneasy? Have you told someone else about this?
- Are you kept informed of stress factors which may adversely affect students in your charge? Is there someone with whom you can share your stress factors?

General

- If you are seeing a parent or guardian, do you make sure someone knows where and when? Do you always have support available to cope with interviews which might prove difficult? Do you choose a place where you have freedom of movement (i.e. not a trapped position), and where there is a discreet means of summoning help?
- Are the emergency procedures working? Do you know what they are, and are they re-assessed regularly?
- Have you ever asked for expert advice (your union, Health and Safety Officer, community police, appropriate helplines, etc.)?
- Do you report all incidents or near incidents as a matter of routine (it could help others)?
- How aware are you that the equanimity of pupils will be affected if they feel their cultural conventions have been transgressed, however unwittingly (e.g. by gesture, invasion of personal space, etc.)?
- Do you ever suffer from stress, fatigue and poor health? This can diminish your ability to cope with sudden traumas. Do you make space and time for relaxation? Have you made time to re-assess your time management lately?
- Have you ever taken up assertiveness/personal safety-first training to help you take control? It is helpful to realize that when you are doing a job of work, you have a right not to be liked, and still to remain in control.

Do you get downhearted if you feel you have mishandled a situation? If so, are you aware that developing the skills to cope with aggression is a steep learning curve for everyone who works in the education sector, and that it pays not to let oneself get downhearted?

Dedicated to

Suzy Lamplugh
1961–1986

'from the end is the beginning'

Part 1

Introduction

1 Violence in the education sector

The Education Service Advisory Committee (ESAC) of the Health and Safety Commission (HSC) consider and advise on problems which may cause harm to the health and safety of people working in the education sector. They say in the introduction to *Managing Health and Safety in Schools*:

> Ensuring health and safety in schools and colleges is an essential part of any school manager's responsibility. However, this cannot be achieved by one person alone. Overall effective health and safety management, including personal safety and security has to be in place. It also has to reflect the more general aspects of management. It has to be a team effort, with the management as well as each member accepting their responsibilities.[1]

Although the great majority of schools and colleges are safe places for most of the time, and horrific acts of outright violence – although nationally traumatic – are certainly still very rare, the ESAC admit that many staff consider violence at work to be one of the most important problems that they face. An atmosphere of continuing threat can damage morale so that staff do not work well; relations with pupils, parents and colleagues can become strained; the quality of teaching and service provided by education establishments may deteriorate. There is also a continuing financial cost.

The Health and Safety Executive (HSE) have treated the issue of workplace violence as a health and safety issue for many years. They have an active Committee on Violence to Staff, and have issued guidance for numerous employment sectors, together with general guidance for all employers. Trade unions also treat workplace violence as a serious issue. In several employment sectors (including the police and some social services work), workplace violence forms the largest source of injuries to workers. It also causes significant absenteeism in most employment sectors, resulting from minor injuries and from the effects of stress.

Workplace managers and their supporting health and safety professionals should treat workplace violence as a hazard to be dealt with in the same way as other hazards. Workplace violence should not be treated as a special case simply because incidents tend to be investigated by the police rather than environmental health officers or the factory inspectorate.

The HSC have now incorporated the reporting of violent incidents and dangerous occurrences in the workplace into the revised *Reporting of Injuries, Diseases and Dangerous Occurrences Regulations* (RIDDOR).[2] This equates the consequences of workplace violence with the regular cuts, slips, trips and falls which are the cause of most workplace injuries. Responsibility for ensuring personal safety management rests with the employer.

For those who work in education, the employer may be an education authority or a board of governors, or it may be the proprietor of an independent school. The Secondary Heads Association (SHA) says:

> Security in schools is the responsibility of Governing bodies. As Executive Officers, Head and Deputy Heads, Principals and Vice Principals, have a duty to ensure that Governors are advised on the need for policies.[3]

Whoever the employers are, it is their mandatory duty to ensure the health and safety and welfare at work of their employees, and the health and safety of non-employees (e.g. children and students) who are in any way affected by the facilities and activities of the school or college.

The aim should be to establish a culture within the school which recognizes that controlling health and safety, including personal safety risks, is an essential part of everyone's daily life. Schools practising effective personal safety management find that the effects percolate throughout school life. It also encourages personal safety at home and on the road.

Some of the benefits of effective health and safety management are straightforward. Most parents are acutely concerned for the safety of their children and want to be assured that the school has good arrangements. Teachers and other staff also need to be confident that they can rely on well thought through and implemented safety guidelines and systems. Resources will not be wasted, as financial priorities can be related to careful risk assessment.

A wide variety of services and jobs are performed in education. Most of these run the risk of violence against staff. Some members of staff carry out a number of activities, and may therefore face risks from more than one source. Managers will need to look carefully at these tasks and consider which occupational groups will face or are likely to face the greatest problems and suffer consequent stress and probable distress. Lunchtime supervisors, for instance, are often on the receiving end of much aggressive behaviour.

While it is true to say that in society at large, fears about violence exceed actual levels of violence, certain occupations carry a special risk of violent attack. Information about violence in the education sector shows a disturbing pattern of threats, actual physical assaults, and more recently, fatalities.

While all the indicators are of growing violence and/or greater awareness and readiness to report violent incidents, the absence of uniform reporting and monitoring systems makes comparisons over time difficult and unreliable. However, a number of studies have revealed higher than expected levels of violence against staff in the education sector. They show that those attacks which have been highly publicized occurred against a background of widespread physical and verbal attacks on those responsible for some element of education. More alarming still is the finding from a recent survey of Manchester schools by the Association of Teachers and Lecturers (ATL) which suggests that the vast majority of local authority schools have no policy for dealing with abuse of teachers.[4]

These findings are disturbing not only because of the potential for abuse to escalate into serious assaults: apparently minor incidents also provoke fear and anxiety. All those involved in the education sector are adversely affected by a culture of threats and aggression.

Even when teachers and others have been aware of a person's history of violence, reports from those who have been attacked indicate a sense of shock and surprise that the event had actually happened. There seems to be a denial of the potential for violence against them, and it has been suggested that this denial is a coping strategy to prevent workers becoming overwhelmed by fear, and thus feeling ineffective and powerless.

Unfortunately, this approach can also lead staff to underestimate or ignore the risk of attack, and to walk, ill prepared, into very dangerous situations. Failure to anticipate the risk of violence, and lack of preparedness to deal with it, can in itself contribute to the development of aggression into actual physical attack.

The combination of these factors, taken together with the opportunities for violence which occur in individual interviews and consultations, provide powerful arguments for the development and implementation of personal safety strategies for all who work in education.

The effects of violence on staff

When a worker has been threatened or physically attacked, a number of responses are likely. Those who have experienced violence frequently report initial 'freezing' at the moment of attack, closely followed by a sense of shock and surprise. Afterwards, there is usually anger, which may be directed at the attacker, at colleagues or the department in which they work, at senior management, or the local authority.

Sometimes, the anger is directed inwards – there appears to be an unrealistic, and often self-imposed, expectation that as professionals they should have been able to anticipate or prevent the attack, and this brings with it a sense of personal failure at not being able to do so. Some of those attacked report feelings of guilt at 'allowing it to happen' and at the subsequent prosecution by the police of the attacker.

One of the major problems for staff is that the aggression and overt violence can be – and most often are – perpetrated by the children in their care, or the parents of the children in their care. People concerned for young people may well have difficulty in reconciling this with clear evidence that the pupil or the parent views them as unhelpful or controlling. In the ATL survey in Manchester, 43 per cent of primary members have been verbally abused by parents and 29 per cent have felt physically threatened by a parent. One in seven ATL members has been assaulted by pupils. The effects of these acts of violence can be considerable.

The effects of a violent attack can include nausea, headaches, sleeplessness, shakiness and extreme fatigue, as well as the direct physical injuries sustained. The emotional and psychological impact of violence can be profound and long-term. Common responses include a sense of isolation, and problems in decision-making in both personal and professional areas of life.

Fear, anger and feelings of revenge, sadness, betrayal and self-doubt all play their part, with one or more of these being more evident at any one time. The fear of further violence, and lack of confidence in handling potentially violent individuals, can have a serious impact on professional practice. Sudden and unexpected feelings of overwhelming fear are not uncommon.

References

1   Education Service Advisory Committee (1995), *Managing Health and Safety in Schools*, London: HMSO, p. 1.
2   Health and Safety Executive (1996), *Reporting of Injuries, Diseases and Dangerous Occurrences Regulations*, London: HSE.
3   Cooper, K. and Little, D. (1996), *Managing Security in Schools and Colleges*, London: Secondary Heads Association, February, p. 7.
4   Association of Teachers and Lecturers, Manchester Branch (1996), *Survey of Assaults on Teachers in Manchester City Schools*, press release.

Further reading

Education Service Advisory Committee (1990), *Violence to Staff in the Education Sector*, London: Health and Safety Executive.
Education Service Advisory Committee (1992), *The Responsibilities of School Governors for Health and Safety*, London: Health and Safety Executive.

2 The risks in perspective

The high-profile reporting of incidents of violence and the increased aware-ness of employers and employees of the risks at work have both positive and negative effects. We all need to be aware of risks inherent in our life and work if we are to develop safe practices, but such knowledge and awareness can engender fear of violence that is out of all proportion to the risk. In assessing the risks we face, we need to consider evidence from a range of sources, as well as looking critically at our own working environment and practices, if we are to develop a balanced view.

Research findings

In the 1980s, the rise in the number of reported assaults of various kinds on employees in the course of their work outpaced the growth in violent crime in general. During the same period, a series of publications based on the work of a variety of organizations and on research work served as evidence that violence at work was a growing source of concern. Employers' organiza-tions, trade unions, professional bodies and others were all becoming increasingly aware of the problems of violence, the need to prevent them wherever possible, and to deal with them effectively when they occurred.

This general view that violence at work has been increasing is difficult to prove or disprove, however, since there has been an absence of large-scale systematic record-keeping, and increases in recorded attacks could stem from the fact that reporting incidents has become more acceptable, rather than reflecting any actual increase in violence.

The lack of data also makes it difficult to quantify either the levels of violence or any changes or differences from year to year, geographically or in particular occupational groups. Despite these limitations, the following pieces of work have contributed to a growing understanding of the nature, scale and effects of violence at work:

- The TUC's report, *Violence to Staff*, in 1988 highlighted the lack of a comprehensive body of data on violence at work.[1] It then reviewed current initiatives on violence to staff in a range of employment sectors, and showed that awareness of the problem had increased but the nature and extent of the risks to employees was still unclear.
- In 1988, the *British Crime Survey* (BCS) found that teachers, welfare workers and nurses were three times more likely than the average employee to be verbally abused or threatened.[2] Other occupational groups with a similarly increased risk of abuse include managers in the entertainment sector, transport workers, male security guards and librarians.
- In 1989, Phillips et al. found that:

  - 8 per cent of people are likely to suffer an assault on their journey to or from work;
  - 20 per cent are likely to experience an unpleasant incident on their journey;
  - 20 per cent face threatening behaviour;
  - sexual harassment occurs most frequently, with 20 per cent of victims being women in professional occupations where they spend a substantial amount of time away from a base, or workers in shops and offices;
  - the frequency of physical attacks ranges from a relatively low 4 per cent for female office workers to approximately 15 per cent for male professionals who often work away from the office;
  - the incidence of experiencing threatening behaviour varies from 10 per cent among office-based professionals to 33 per cent for those who often meet clients.[3]

- The *British Crime Survey* for 1988 showed that 25 per cent of crime victims said that the incident had happened at, or because of, work.[4] Fourteen per cent of respondents said they had been verbally abused at work at least once in the previous year, and approximately 33 per cent of all threats of violence were received at work.
- Research published in 1987 by the Labour Research Department was largely concerned with public services, and showed that:

  - 98 per cent of workplaces had experienced instances of abuse or harassment;
  - 85 per cent of workplaces reported that threats of violence had been made;

- 62 per cent of workplaces suffered one or more instances of actual violence, including 80 per cent of transport companies and 77 per cent of health authorities;
- 28 per cent of workplaces had experienced violence using a weapon.[5]

In the survey of 210 workplaces with a total of over 86,000 employees, 67 per cent felt that the level of abuse and violence had increased during the past five years.

The risk of crime

While fear of crime is understandable – because of what we see and hear in the media, or as a result of having been subjected to violence or living in an area of high levels of crime – it is important to place the risks in perspective. In many cases, the fear of crime is disproportionate to the actual risk. A Home Office study on *fear of crime* shows that the perceived level of crime sometimes bears little resemblance to the true level, especially crimes of violence and sexual offences.[6] People very often overestimate the risk of crimes of violence. Similarly, the proportion of all crimes that involve violence is generally overestimated.

The Home Office study and other similar work demonstrate that crimes of violence against the person represent only a small proportion of all crimes. The chance of an individual being a victim of violent crime is far less than the chance of them being a victim of car crime. However, it is important to remember that:

- Even a small percentage of a total of 5.5 million crimes in general means there were 295,000 individual violent crimes in England and Wales in 1993.
- Although a crime may not involve violence against the person within the legal definition, it may still result in the individual feeling attacked and violated.
- Many incidents of violence at work go unreported in the workplace, let alone to the police.
- The crime statistics can only indicate the statistical probability of being a victim of violent crime; they do not take account of individuals at greater risk because of the work they do or their lifestyle.
- Outside domestic violence, violent crime is not the issue it is sometimes assumed to be, that is, that women are more at risk than men. In fact, many more subjects of violent crime are men rather than women, and the majority of assaults are by young men on young men.

Sexual offences

In a previous book in this series, Pauline Bibby[7] showed that in the year to June 1993, the police in England and Wales recorded 29,618 sexual offences, 0.5 per cent of the total of all crimes. This figure represented a fall in the number of offences of 125 over the previous 12 months' recorded sexual offences. Table 2.1 shows the figures for the different categories of sexual offences as a percentage of the total of all sexual offences.

Table 2.1   Breakdown of sexual offences by category

Offence	%
Buggery	4.0
Indecent assault on a male	10.5
Indecency between males	2.5
Rape	14.5
Unlawful sexual intercourse	6.1
Indecent assault on a female	55.5
Incest	1.2
Procuration	0.5
Abduction	1.1
Bigamy	0.3
Gross indecency with a child	3.9

Source: Home Office Research and Statistics Department (1993), *British Crime Survey*, London: HMSO.

However, more recent figures published in April 1994 do show a 6 per cent increase in reported sexual offences, to 31,400.[8] Greater willingness to report such offences may be contributing to this increase in numbers.

As well as crime figures, other statistical information helps to put the risk of becoming the subject of a sexual offence into perspective. For example:

● About 40 per cent of rapes take place between people already known to each other.
● Over 60 per cent of rapes take place in buildings, homes and offices, rather than in the dark alleys we hear of in the more sensational press.

- Sexual offences against males are far more common than most people believe.
- You are more likely to become a rape victim between the ages of 16 and 24, and least likely under 10 years of age or over 60.
- The majority of convicted rapists are men in their twenties.
- Contrary to popular belief about night-time risks, many assaults and attacks take place in the afternoon.
- Statistically, any individual's chance of becoming a victim of a sexual offence is low, but other factors such as lifestyle, geographical location and occupation can change the probability.[9]

Information of this sort can help in allaying unnecessary fears while enabling people to recognize real risks and thereafter make sensible arrangements that will help to keep them safe. For example:

- Women should not assume that they are safe because they are meeting a man they know through work, particularly if they will be on his premises.
- Men should not assume they are safe from sexual offences simply because they are men.

References

1 Trades Union Congress (1988), *Violence to Staff: Progress Report*, London: TUC .
2 Home Office Research and Statistics Department (1988), *British Crime Survey*, London: HMSO.
3 Phillips, C.M., Stockdale, J.E. and Joeman, L.M. (1989), *The Risks of Going to Work*, London: The Suzy Lamplugh Trust.
4 Home Office Research and Statistics Department, op. cit.
5 Labour Research Department (1987), *Assaults on Staff – Bargaining Report*, London: LRD, July.
6 Home Office Public Relations Branch (1984), *Fear of Crime in England and Wales, Report of the Working Group*, London: Home Office Public Relations Branch.
7 Bibby, P. (1995), *Personal Safety for Health Care Workers*, Aldershot: Arena.
8 Consumers' Association (1990), 'Which? Report on Street Crime', *Which?*, November, pp. 636–9.
9 Ibid.

Further reading

Cardy, C. (1992), *Training for Personal Safety at Work*, Aldershot: Connaught Training.

3 Schools and their communities

School life is affected by all the factors which affect children and their parents. The challenges facing schools in the 1990s are made more acute by the fact that children and young people bring with them into the classroom, playground, playing fields, and into their interpersonal relations, the problems, distress and expectations of their parents and carers, all compounded by the circumstances and conditions of the community and the world at large, which are out of their control. The National Union of Teachers (NUT) states in its document, *Security, Schools and the Community*:

> the prevailing mood of the community affects the schools within it. Where there is a climate of violence and fear, that will impinge upon the school. The line between the community and school is difficult to draw.[1]

Violence in families

Undoubtedly, violence in families presents the greatest problem, both for schools and society as a whole. In 1993, the Gulbenkian Foundation convened a commission to review what is known about the development of violent attitudes of children, and what triggers their involvement in violent actions.

The commission's findings, published by the Gulbenkian Foundation in 1995 in a comprehensive report entitled *Children and Violence*, were that children become violent as a result of:

- the violence meted out to them by their parents or carers;
- violent and humiliating forms of discipline from parents and carers;
- frequent and excessive demonstrations of parental anger;
- inconsistency on the part of parents as to what constitutes wrongdoing;
- neglect which leads to the inadequate monitoring and supervision of children.[2]

Those who work with children know that physical assault, emotional deprivation, physical neglect, inadequate supervision and sexual exploitation are all too often suffered by children in the context of their families.

Bullying, verbal abuse and violent behaviour are without doubt part and parcel of normal existence for some children. In the context of the home, they learn that violence and aggression can be tools for getting one's own way, imposing one's will on others. Where alcohol is involved, such situations inevitably become much worse. Since those who suffer most often from domestic violence are usually women and children, and the perpetrators are usually male, the lesson is not lost on the children, especially boys.

The deterioration in the quality of family life, marital breakdown and the increase in violence in general has been noted in schools up and down the country. At a conference organized by The Suzy Lamplugh Trust in 1995, 'Youth of Britain: Personal Safety Matters!', one of the speakers was the head of a nursery school established by Bedfordshire County Council for working parents and families with special needs. This speaker painted a worrying picture of the increase of aggression in her nursery school:

> Over the past few years we have become increasingly concerned about the aggressive, non-verbal communication between children. There is the thump before you even try to say anything, it's the silent challenge, the scowling look, the biting, the head butting – and these are serious attacks. These are not pulled punches in a game.[3]

As many teachers know, such situations are not unusual, and teachers have to bring ever greater effort, time and resources to bear upon these problems, in order to ensure schools remain non-violent places. Indeed, without great vigilance on the part of teachers and other staff, without effective anti-bullying policies and forms of mediation, including peer mediation, schools themselves may be the context for bullying, harassment, intimidation, fights and other forms of violence.

But anti-social tendencies in children do not always stem from poor family background or poor parental example. Children can also become disruptive because they suffer from undiagnosed learning difficulties. They may be hampered by dyslexia, deafness, visual impairment, aphasia, and so on. Indeed, non-conformity to the 'norm' is a factor in creating targets for bullying. Even those who are very bright or speak differently can be singled out and react accordingly. In most of these cases, disruptive children are demonstrating by their behaviour their frustration, anger, distress and usually deep unhappiness. Such feelings can, in turn, provoke acts of violence. The result may well be expulsion from school.

Expulsion from school

Whereas pupils aged 14–16 were once thought to be the most difficult age group, children of all ages are now to be found among those considered disruptive, and permanent exclusions from school have been rising steadily in the 1990s, in both the primary and secondary school sectors. Experienced teachers attest to the increase in abusive behaviour to which they and other children are subjected.

Once outside the school, disaffected pupils can become marauders of the school which has discarded them. Considering themselves unappreciated, determined to prove they are somebody, they will frequently join a gang and be drawn into criminal activities.

Teenage views on violence and aggression

At a recent conference, a young teacher said he still found it difficult to understand that young people seemed to take the present level of crime in their stride. They just appeared to accept violence, the use of drugs, overuse of alcohol, shoplifting, burglary and the break-up of marriages as inevitable. By the time they are 21, 1 in 3 young men will have a criminal record.

A recent survey carried out by Stephen Jarrett for The Suzy Lamplugh Trust[4] among 14- and 15-year-olds who were following one of the Trust's personal safety programmes, found that:

- Most thought that 90 per cent of violent situations occur on the street or in public places, and the perpetrators were almost always young men.
- The majority felt these violent incidents were not preventable (at the same time, all thought that youths do not behave violently at home or in front of parents).
- Fifty per cent of the boys felt violence against other teenagers was inevitable.
- The reasons for bullying or violent behaviour were given as: peer pressure, being bullied at home, boredom and frustration on the streets, vandalism, drug-taking and stealing.
- Forty per cent said they knew of a violent adult.

However, contrary to the perceptions of the young teacher mentioned earlier, many thought violence was unacceptable:

- The majority felt it unacceptable for a teenager to hit an adult.
- Almost all were against hitting animals, but the girls felt it all right to hit children as a means of discipline.

- 50% thought violence towards a child by an adult should be reported, and the child should be legally protected.

In discussion, it also became clear that many young people were well aware of the drug-pushers within the education environment, the teenagers who are thieving, the older man who is targeting young girls, and the so-called 'uncle' who is using his friend's son to seek out young boys. In many of these situations, they would have liked to pass on this information, but they were frightened, sometimes suffering actual physical and mental intimidation. The result was that they did not want to get involved, did not want to be interviewed by the police, did not want their details taken down, and certainly did not want to be a witness. Some were frightened, not only for themselves, but for their families as well.

Many, however, know right from wrong and wish to be good citizens. The guilt, fear and the stress which stems from the non-disclosure of what they know can result in considerable strain, tension and even depression. Yet Crimestoppers is a useful and anonymous way whereby these young people could fulfil a valuable public service. (See Appendix B.)

Teenage attitudes to safety

Children learn much from observing adult behaviour and attitudes and, as already noted, the messages which they receive from adults about violence appear ambivalent, none more so than those which concern adult fears about crime.

To children, grown-ups either seem fearful, or they express the view that only strong-arm tactics will protect them. It follows that children must learn 'to stick up for themselves'.

The effect of these views may be to cause young people to carry weapons. This was recently confirmed by a survey in youth clubs undertaken by a Suzy Lamplugh Trust trainer.[5] Among the more disturbing findings were the following:

- All respondents said they carried something that could be used as a weapon.
- All said they carried the weapon in case they needed to use it in 'self-defence'. (One of the objects was a piece of wood with a huge nail hammered through the middle.)
- None of the respondents informed their parents truthfully of their whereabouts.
- Despite the perceived need to carry weapons, all the boys thought girls were more at risk than they were (in fact, most assaults are by young men on other young men).

- Forty per cent of boys had been attacked.
- All had been harassed by other people.
- All had friends who travelled alone in the dark, late at night.
- All had been warned by police that in carrying a weapon for so-called 'self-defence', they risked having it used against them, and that if they used it on someone else, a long prison sentence was the likely result.
- All had reacted negatively to this warning.

Such a situation is scarcely surprising, since in relatively few schools do pupils receive positive personal safety programmes as part of their curriculum entitlement. Yet all the evidence suggests that children who lack personal safety skills and strategies remain vulnerable children. Vulnerable children become frightened, insecure teenagers. And such teenagers are, as we have recently seen, tempted to carry weapons, with tragic consequences.

Schools can help

It was the view of the Gulbenkian Foundation's Commission on Children and Violence that despite all the difficulties which schools face, there is much good which schools do to ameliorate the damaging effects which poor living conditions and violent demonstrations of parental anger can have on a child.[6] In fact, schools and colleges are the only organizations which can ensure that all children and young people receive programmes through which they will learn to reduce and prevent violence, and more importantly, control their own aggression.

The Gulbenkian Foundation report states that all schools need programmes which teach children 'that violence is abnormal and unacceptable; that hitting skills and social skills are mutually exclusive and cannot co-exist. Children, like adults, hit out when they have nothing better left in their social vocabulary.'

The Suzy Lamplugh Trust's position

Following the disappearance and presumed murder of Suzy Lamplugh in 1986, the parents of the missing estate agent set up the national charity for personal safety which bears her name. The Suzy Lamplugh Trust began its work by researching and by providing training resources to combat the problem of violence in the workplace. It was soon realized that this work needed to commence at school, and ten years on, personal safety resources have been made available for both primary and secondary schools.[7,8]

Trials of these resources in schools revealed unexpected benefits, such as helping bullies to stop bullying; teaching those who were being bullied to become more assertive and more confident, and enabling some students to reveal more serious abuse to which they had been subjected, often over a number of years. Others came forward with what can best be termed 'near misses' to their safety.

Perhaps the greatest benefit was a clearer understanding of aggression and violence by the young participants, and their realization that in the long term, aggression not only has no place in a civilized society, it is extremely counter-productive.

If positive steps are to be taken to reduce the aggression in society and to enable citizens to lead safer, more confident lives, all schools will need to provide children with repeated and developmentally appropriate opportunities to acquire sound personal safety skills. Safety programmes will always be more effective if parents are encouraged to play an active role in helping schools to implement child safety programmes and in reinforcing their children's new-found skills. It is not unknown for parents to learn personal safety skills from their children.

This can only be achieved if personal safety is perceived as an issue which involves and affects everyone who works or learns within the institution – teaching and non-teaching staff alike. Personal safety education implies, by definition, an identifiable and widely accepted ethos of respect for the rights and well-being of others. As such, it is an essential part of the personal and social education of every child.

References

1   National Union of Teachers (1996), *Security, Schools and the Community*, London: NUT.
2   Gulbenkian Foundation (1995), *Children and Violence*, London: Calouste Gulbenkian Foundation.
3   Suzy Lamplugh Trust (1995), *Youth of Britain: Personal Safety Matters! Report of the Suzy Lamplugh Trust Conference, 17 January 1995*, London: The Suzy Lamplugh Trust, p. 12.
4   Jarrett, Stephen (1995), 'Survey: Studies in Teenage Attitudes to Safety', *Youth of Britain: Personal Safety Matters! Report of the Suzy Lamplugh Trust Conference, 17 January 1995*, London: The Suzy Lamplugh Trust, p. 19.
5   Ibid.
6   Gulbenkian Foundation, op. cit.
7   Suzy Lamplugh Trust (1995), *Home Safe*, London: The Suzy Lamplugh Trust.
8   Suzy Lamplugh Trust (1991, 1994), *Well Safe* (secondary schools resource pack), London: The Suzy Lamplugh Trust.

Part 2

Responsibilities of governors,
employers and managers

4 Violence at work

In Part 1, we have endeavoured to set the present picture of violence against staff in the education sector in the wider context of the whole community and the problems of the individual, as well as the so-called 'culture of violence'. There are very real concerns; there are also useful answers. Many of the ideas in this book may seem to be just common sense.

This part of the book discusses the evidence, definition and risk assessment of violence which is most relevant to those working in education, whatever their role.

Statistics and research on workplace violence

Until the April 1996 introduction of reporting in RIDDOR,[1] there was no centralized system to gather statistics on workplace violence in the UK. Most serious violent crime is dealt with by the various police services around the country, who investigate incidents with a view to criminal prosecution. Verbal abuse generally receives little attention. Health and safety statistics have not contained any specific reference to workplace violence. There has been little investigation of the possible workplace factors in the incidents which result in claims from the Criminal Injuries Compensation Agency.

Several reports, including the paper produced by the Loss Prevention Council on violence at work,[2] have been published in the UK. Most of the statistical information has resulted from survey work, rather than incident analysis. A review of some of this data appeared in the *British Crime Survey*,[3] which, among other matters, looked at violent assaults, threats and thefts for a sample of 10,000 people, and calculated estimated averages for the whole population. The 1988 survey noted that about 25 per cent of all violent assaults and about 30 per cent of all threats made against working people occur while at work. Occupations particularly noted for violent assaults and threats were welfare workers, nurses, security personnel and entertainment (pub) managers. Teachers were also deemed to be prone to verbal threats and physical violence.

The Home Office 1993 study on the 1992 *British Crime Survey* noted several other interesting features.[4] Roughly a quarter of violent assaults at work involved other people who worked there; the rest were perpetrated by members of the public. Fewer than 20 per cent of offenders were said to be drunk. Only 31 per cent of assaults were committed by strangers: most assailants were known well or by sight. Most of those assaulted were in the 16–29 age range, whereas half of the offenders in the workplace were estimated to be over 25, compared to one third for all assaults in general. As with most violent assaults, the evening was the time of greatest risk, but workplace assaults could occur at any time of day. Only a third of offences were reported to the police. Only about 10 per cent of victims saw a doctor, and the same proportion felt that they were in some way responsible for what happened.

The most worrisome feature is that the workplace seems to be the fastest-growing of all locations for violent crime. Between 1981 and 1991, the annual rate of violent assaults at work more than doubled, to 350,000 incidents. These accounted for over 13 per cent of all assaults. This trend can certainly be noted in schools and colleges.[5]

The report commissioned by The Suzy Lamplugh Trust in 1989 concentrated specifically on workplace violence.[6] This work again identified specific groups of workers at risk, situations where violence occurs, and listed many simple risk improvements which could be adopted by responsible employers. The report also revealed that awareness of the issue of workplace violence is increasing, and that many employers were already acting on this.

This research concluded that:

- Violence at work is an issue for both employers and employees.
- It is widespread – not confined to 'women's work' or to the UK.
- Perceptions of risk do not always match reality.
- Anxiety is no substitute for action. Institutional provision is crucial to employees' safety – all too often, action only follows a serious incident.
- Violence at work has high costs to both the individual and the organization.
- Young males are the group most vulnerable to physical attack in the course of work.

The Elton Report

As a result of public concern about violence and discipline in schools, an independent committee of inquiry into school discipline in England and

Wales, chaired by Lord Elton, was set up by the government in March 1988. The committee published its report – the Elton Report – in March 1989.[7]

The Elton Committee was concerned mainly with discipline in schools, but it did consider problems of violence and physical aggression. A survey to examine teachers' perceptions and concerns about discipline found that of approximately 2,500 secondary school teachers surveyed during one week, 15 per cent (1 in 7) of teachers had suffered verbal abuse, and that overall, about 0.5 per cent (one in 200) teachers had experienced incidents of a clearly violent nature.

Although the committee concluded at that time that actual physical attacks by pupils on members of staff were rare, such attacks were regarded as a very serious matter. Teaching staff in mainstream schools were the principal subjects of Elton's inquiry, but the risk of violence also exists for many other groups of employees in the education sector. Unfortunately, there is little or no statistical information available on these other groups.

Some teaching unions commissioned surveys of their members which produced disturbing figures about the levels of threatening behaviour and physical violence suffered by schoolteachers, often at the hands of pupils. These surveys have also highlighted the level of concern felt by staff about actual and potential violence in schools and colleges.

If the 1996 ALT survey[8] on violence and aggression faced by teachers in Manchester were true of the UK as a whole then, since 1989, the proportion of teachers suffering verbal abuse has risen from 15 per cent to 43 per cent, and assaults on teachers have risen from 0.5 per cent to 15 per cent. There has been a marked deterioration in the 1990s.

Violence in the education sector needs to be dealt with actively. Local education authorities (LEAs) and other education employers (including sub-contractors working at education premises) need to take positive steps towards reducing and combating the risks of violence to their staff.

Defining violence and aggression

The first step in developing a personal safety strategy is for the organization to produce working definitions to clarify what is being addressed. Violence and aggression are often spoken of as if it is perfectly clear what they are – indeed, the two terms are often used interchangeably. Individual perceptions of violence and aggression differ, however. It is all too easy to assume that there is some shared, readily understood concept of such behaviour, as well as common knowledge of the scale of violence and aggression at work and elsewhere.

Just as perceptions of violence vary, so do reactions. Some staff do not acknowledge violence as a problem in their job, while others may be anxious to the extent of being unable to carry out their professional tasks effectively.

Dictionary definitions focus on the words and what they mean in an objective, academic sense. They tell us something of what is generally understood by the terms 'violence' and 'aggression'. But such definitions do not touch on the causes or effects of aggression and violence, nor how to recognize either of these in an organizational or work context.

There have been attempts to produce 'working' definitions, and these generally seek to describe the behavioural characteristics associated with aggression and violence and their effects. Some examples of 'working' definitions are:

- 'Any incident in which an employee is abused, threatened or assaulted by a member of the public in circumstances arising out of the course of his or her employment.' (Health and Safety Executive's working definition of violence, 1988)[9]
- 'The application of force, severe threat or serious abuse by members of the public towards people arising out of the course of their work whether or not they are on duty. This includes severe verbal abuse or threat where this is judged likely to turn into actual violence; serious or persistent harassment (including racial or sexual harassment); threat with a weapon; major or minor injuries; fatalities.'[10]
- 'Behaviour which produces damaging or hurtful effects, physically or emotionally, on people.'[11]

These working definitions widen the dictionary definitions to encompass verbal aggression or abuse, threat or harassment. They also attempt to describe the behaviour associated with aggression and violence, as well as its effects on the person attacked.

Seeking a definition may seem rather pedantic, but it is an important, although often forgotten, basic step in addressing problems of aggression and violence at work for the following reasons:

- We need to know what it is we are talking about and trying to manage. Many people still assume violence only includes serious physical attack, rape and murder. In practice, a wide range of behaviour is now recognized as violent or aggressive and appreciated as being damaging to individual employees and the work of the organization. The range of behaviour includes:

Physical violence

- assault causing death
- assault causing serious physical injury

Non-physical violence

- verbal abuse
- racial or sexual abuse

- minor injuries
- kicking
- biting
- punching
- use of weapons
- use of missiles
- spitting
- scratching
- sexual assault
- deliberate self-harm

- threats – with or without weapons
- physical posturing
- threatening gestures
- abusive 'phone calls
- threatening use of dogs
- swearing
- shouting
- name-calling
- bullying
- insults
- innuendo
- deliberate silence.

- Developing a definition should take into account the context and culture of the organization and the characteristics of the staff and the potential aggressors. Considering the contextual issues in developing a definition helps to ensure that it is workable because it encompasses what the organization (both employers and employees) believes to be violent behaviour, as opposed to behaviour resulting from other factors.

- Perceptions of aggression and violence will vary between those who have experienced violence and those who have not, and between people at high risk and people at much less risk. Not everyone will be equally vulnerable or resilient when it comes to dealing with violence or the fear of it. A process of involving people means working to bring perceptions into the open, so that they can be taken into account in developing a definition to which everyone can subscribe. Thus it is important to involve locally-based and centrally-based staff, as well as professional associations and trade unions, in arriving at agreed working definitions.

- A definition, although artificial in some ways, can be shared, explained and understood, thereby establishing a basis for recognizing violence and aggression. General understanding can significantly increase people's willingness to report incidents. Under-reporting of incidents has been a serious problem that many believe results from a lack of confidence that reports of violence will be perceived by others as the person attacked perceives them. The dismissing of reports as 'part of the job' or evidence of over-sensitivity on the part of the employee has been all too common. Occasionally, in education, 'concern for the child' can be a motive in not reporting aggression by the parents. Consequences need to be considered in a wider context.

Developing a working definition of 'aggression' and 'violence' for the organization is therefore an important foundation of understanding upon which to build commitment, policy, procedures and working practices.

It does not matter whether someone else's definition is used as a starting point or the process is begun with a blank sheet of paper. Whether aggressive behaviour and violent behaviour are defined separately, or 'violence' is used as a term to cover a continuum of behaviour (as many organizations do) is not critical. Nor does it matter whether the definition sounds learned or is a straightforward list of behaviour included within the definition.

What does matter is that the definition is developed in such a way that it is shared and so can inform the future behaviour and perceptions of everyone. This implies consultation with the workforce, specifically those people most likely to be at risk, rather than the imposition of a definition by policy-makers or others relatively remote from the 'front line'. This may appear a long-winded and time-consuming way of arriving at a form of words, but it is well worth doing, as it can cover a good deal of the groundwork necessary to develop a policy.

Throughout the remainder of this book, the use of the term 'victim' of violence has been kept to a minimum. It is important to avoid any tendency to stigmatize those who have been on the receiving end of violence and aggression. Rather, the focus needs to be on encouraging employers to take responsibility for seeing that staff are positively supported in dealing with issues of violence.

Violence at work has been defined by the HSE, pressure groups and other bodies. Most agree on a wide definition, which includes verbal abuse as well as actual physical assault, and this is the one which we use in this book.

It must be appreciated that there may also be a risk from fellow members of staff. The HSE's definition of violence does not extend to violence between employees. Such bullying can be more insidious, and should warrant equivalent or greater scrutiny from employers. 'Victimization' is another word used in this context, normally describing verbal or psychological abuse by management or colleagues. Contractors and visitors would come under the heading of 'members of the public'.

For the purposes of this book, a 'workplace assault' is defined as an act of violence which results in physical injury to the employee. Physical injuries can take many forms, including homicide. Psychological injury may also occur with a physical injury, and may occur on its own without an assault. This will generally take the form of acute stress reactions or post-traumatic stress disorder.

The process of arriving at a definition of violence which is agreed by all concerned will result in:

- raising awareness at all levels;
- attention to the ways in which the work setting itself can be adapted or better managed to reduce risk;
- agreement on appropriate methods for responding to violent incidents.

This, in turn, will highlight the need for appropriate training and support for staff and management.

References

1 Health and Safety Executive (1996), *Reporting of Injuries, Diseases and Dangerous Occurrences Regulations*, London: HSE.
2 Hodge, J. (1995), *Loss Prevention Council – Technical Briefing Note for Insurers – Violence at Work*, London: HSE.
3 Home Office Research and Statistics Department (1988), *British Crime Survey*, London: HMSO.
4 Mayhew, P., Aye Maung, N. and Mirrlees-Black, C. (1993), *The 1992 British Crime Survey*, Home Office Research Study No. 132, London: HMSO.
5 Ibid.
6 Phillips, C.M., Stockdale J.E. and Joeman, L.M. (1989), *The Risks in Going to Work*, London: The Suzy Lamplugh Trust.
7 Elton Committee (1989), *Discipline in Schools – Report of the Committee of Inquiry Chaired by Lord Elton* (The Elton Report), HMSO.
8 Association of Teachers and Lecturers, Manchester Branch (1996), *Survey of Assaults on Teachers in Manchester City Schools*, press release.
9 Health and Safety Executive (1988), *Preventing Violence to Staff*, London: HMSO.
10 Department of Health and Social Security Advisory Committee on Violence to Staff (1988), *Violence to Staff*, London: HMSO.
11 Association of Directors of Social Services (1987), *Guidelines and Recommendations to Employers on Violence against Employees in the Personal Social Services*, Worcester: ADSS.

5 Employer and employee roles

Despite the clear duties and obligations placed on employers and employees, some institutions still have very limited arrangements for tackling the problem of potential violence. Some institutions, especially in the private sector, have no arrangements at all.

Recent tragic incidents in or near educational establishments can have left no one in any doubt that there is an urgent need to set in place security arrangements which will help to protect schools from random acts of violence which emanate from outside the school and where perpetrators may or may not have connections with the school.

The legal duty of the employer

Section 2 (1) of the Health and Safety at Work Act 1974 (HSW Act) imposes a general obligation and specific applications of the Act upon employers.[1] The general obligation is:

> It shall be the duty of every employer to ensure so far as is reasonably practicable, the health, safety and welfare of all employees.

The matters to which that duty extends include:

- 'The provision and maintenance of plant and systems of work that are, so far as is reasonably practicable, safe and without risk to health';
- 'The provision of such information, instruction, training and supervision as is necessary to ensure, so far as is reasonably practicable, the health and safety at work of employees';
- 'The provision and maintenance of a working environment for employees that is, so far as is reasonably practicable, safe and without risk to health'.

In addition, there is an obligation to draw up and publish written safety policies to include these matters. Apart from the obligations under the HSW Act, there are other obligations on an employer arising from:

- the employer's duty of care under Common Law for the safety of employees;
- the employer's duty under any nationally negotiated agreements;
- the employer's duty not to dismiss employees unfairly; employees have resigned in some situations and successfully alleged constructive dismissal because the employer failed to provide reasonable precautions for the employee's safety.

Employers face penalties under the HSW Act if they fail to meet their obligations. Employees also have the option of seeking other remedies where any employer fails to fulfil his or her duty including damages, industrial action and resignation, followed by a claim for constructive unfair dismissal.

The key question arising from this is: What is meant by 'reasonably practicable'? The meaning is largely governed by case law, of which the most important example is a Court of Appeal case, *Edwards* v. *National Coal Board* (1949), IKB 704. In giving judgment, Lord Justice Asquith said:

> 'reasonably practicable' is a narrower term than 'physically possible' and seems to me to imply that a computation must be made by the owner in which the quantum of risk is placed on one scale and the sacrifice involved in the measures necessary for averting the risk (whether in money, time or trouble) is placed in the other.

The principles of this case would apply to proceedings under the HSW Act or any similar proceedings. This means that:

- the burden of proof that all reasonably practicable measures have been taken rests upon the employer; employers must be able to show that they had applied their minds to the computation mentioned by Lord Justice Asquith;
- courts will decide, on the factual evidence, whether the employers are entitled to rely upon the 'reasonably practicable' defence.

These principles have been upheld in a number of cases arising from areas of employment as varied as local authorities, mining and the entertainment industry. In other cases, the judges have made it clear that there is a requirement on employers to:

- take action to minimize risks to employees;
- take into account the risk of criminal attack, as part of the obligation to provide a safe system of work.

The HSW Act can be enforced:

- by an Improvement Notice, when an inspector considers health and safety legislation is being contravened;
- by a Prohibition Notice, when an inspector considers there is a risk of serious personal injury;
- by prosecution for breach of the HSW Act or its relevant statutory provisions.

A breach of Sections 2–6 of the HSW Act is liable to a £20,000 fine; breach of other relevant statutory provisions, £5,000. Magistrates may imprison, for up to six months, individuals who fail to comply with an Improvement or Prohibition Notice; in the Crown Court, the maximum period is two years.

In addition, the HSC have made serious workplace violence (over three-day injuries, where an employee is incapacitated for more than three consecutive days) a specific type of incident which must be reported under RIDDOR.[2] This imposes a legal reporting duty on employers. Employers should set up their reporting systems for workplace violence in advance of this possible requirement. The requirement to report injuries affecting members of the public may also be widened. This may induce members of the public to bring claims against organizations, with implications for general liability.

In their consultation document on the proposed changes to RIDDOR, the Health and Safety Commission estimated that about 1,000 extra reports would emerge each year because of a requirement to report certain violent acts.[3] This may be an underestimate, as the annual incidence reported in the 1988 British Crime Survey is around 350,000.[4]

Another aspect of the HSW Act is sometimes forgotten – the duty it places upon individuals. In Section 7 of the Act, it is made clear that it is the

> duty of every employee to take reasonable care for the health and safety of himself and other people who may be affected by his act or omissions at work.

Of particular interest is Section 37 which stipulates that offences under the Act may be committed either by individual people or by corporate bodies such as limited companies, nationalized industries or local authorities. If an offence committed by a corporate body was committed with the consent or connivance of a director, manager, secretary or other officer, or because of their negligence, that party is also guilty of the offence, and may be prosecuted as well as the corporate body. Although prosecutions of individuals under this provision have been rare, it is well worth managers and others remembering its existence and the implications for them personally.

The balance struck within the Act between employer and employee responsibility is extremely important. It is pointless for an employer to develop safe working practices if members of the workforce do not observe the rules of safe working, fail to follow the procedures laid down, or otherwise put themselves and/or others at risk. Similarly, an employee can strive to work safely, but his/her ability to do so can be severely limited without the commitment and support of the employer, or if the guidelines are not appropriate.

Some of the general duties under the HSW Act have been supplemented by the Management of Health and Safety at Work Regulations 1992,[5] which implement the EC Framework Directive on Health and Safety. The regulations require that employers undertake a systematic general examination of their work activities and record significant findings of their assessment. Also under the 1992 regulations a risk assessment must identify:

- the extent and nature of the risk;
- the factors which contribute to the risk;
- the causes, and the changes necessary to eliminate or control the risk.

Clearly, assessments will vary according to the type of work involved, the location and working patterns. Reviews of any guidelines should be conducted at regular intervals, and should form part of standard management practice.

The costs of violence

It is not only the statutory responsibility or other imposed obligations that provide the motivation to develop safe working practices. There are personal and organizational costs associated with violence in the workplace. Personal attack or injury can lead to staff absences on sick leave, as a result of the injury itself or the psychological damage caused by it, which may lead to depression, insomnia, agoraphobia or panic attacks. The employer may face litigation costs or insurance claims, which in turn lead to higher insurance costs, and an attack is likely to lead to bad publicity for the school itself.

Employee effectiveness is likely to be reduced by loss of confidence, anxiety and stress, and may involve fear of certain aspects of work. This stress can present a double effect, combined with the post-traumatic stress syndrome which nearly everyone consciously or unconsciously experiences when they are threatened or frightened, even if no physical attack has taken place.

PTSD (post-trauma stress disorder) is now a well documented and recognized condition which can severely affect whether or not employees can continue to work. Skilled professional counselling may be necessary to enable sufferers to regain their former mental balance and energies. Work-related stress is also now an accepted condition which is taken seriously by employers. What is less obvious is that employees subjected to such obvious forms of aggression as snide comments and verbal abuse, or the less frequent sexual threats, invitations or innuendo, can suffer considerably from stress-related problems.

Women employees faced with these kinds of aggression are likely to seek help and advice. But, for men, self-image can exacerbate these problems. It may be difficult for a man to return to the staffroom and admit he cannot cope with the situation he faces, especially one in which he may have been sexually taunted by female students.

Any form of violence, whether or not it results in some sort of physical injury, can have serious adverse effects on the workforce, including:

- high levels of anxiety;
- stress-related illness;
- absenteeism and the need to cover for staff;
- low morale;
- high levels of staff turnover;
- low productivity;
- little job satisfaction;
- low employee involvement;
- industrial action or poor industrial relations;
- difficulty in recruiting and retaining staff.

So far as the education service is concerned, there is an additional factor to be taken into account. By the nature of the work they do, staff in education have a responsibility for the health and safety – including personal safety – of the young people in their care.

To fulfil these obligations, all educational establishments need to draw up a statement of intent, followed by a plan of action and a written safety policy and procedures, including the reporting of 'near misses'.

Statement of intent

As stated above, there is a requirement in law following the Management of Health and Safety at Work Regulations 1992 that all employers who have five or more employees must carry out risk assessment processes and record their findings. Under the regulations, which came into effect in January 1993, employers must 'ensure a safe place of work'. This duty is wide in scope, and extends to the protection of staff against violent incidents, where these are foreseeable. Section 2 implies that an employer should consider not only the threat of actual injury, but also the potential effects of employees' physical and mental health or welfare, for example if subjected to continuous verbal abuse.

The National Association of Head Teachers has issued a very clear definition of who is responsible:

> It is clear from the Health and Safety at Work Act that health and safety responsibilities lie with the employer. Those who have a responsibility can delegate the tasks necessary to discharge the responsibility but they cannot delegate the responsibility itself.[6]

In different types of school, the legal situation is as follows:

- **County and controlled schools** – 'The introduction of Local Management has not changed the legal responsibilities of the LEA under the Health and Safety at Work Acts. Heads must be familiar with and respond to the LEA policy on Health and Safety.'
- **Aided schools** – 'As the governing body is the employer, it has responsibility under the Health and Safety at Work Act. It should seek advice and assistance about the nature of its responsibilities from both the Diocese and the LEA.'
- **Grant-maintained schools, city technology colleges and independent schools** – 'The governing body is responsible in law for all aspects of health and safety. It must establish a clear health and safety policy.'
- **All other establishments** – 'Members in educational establishments falling outside the three categories identified above, are advised to ensure they have a clear understanding as to where their responsibilities lie.'[7]

The NAHT also point out that:

> Whilst the responsibility for health and safety cannot be delegated to individual schools, Local Authorities will delegate the enactment of their responsibility to schools. Members will therefore find themselves responsible for ensuring, as a management task, that the procedures for risk assessment have been fully and appropriately undertaken. In a similar way, governors in grant maintained, aided and independent schools will delegate enactment to the head teacher.[8]

Section 2(3) of the HSW Act requires employers to prepare a written health and safety policy statement. This should include the organization and arrangements for dealing with foreseeable risks of violence to staff. When incident-reporting procedures and a preventive strategy have been discussed, devised and agreed by the employer and employees or their representatives, these should be incorporated into the safety policy.

Employers also have HSW Act responsibilities to people working at their premises who are not their employees – for example, contract cleaning or catering staff. In these circumstances, the LEA or governing body will need to liaise with the employer of the contract staff to discuss how both can best deal with risks of violence to their staff, reporting procedures for incidents, etc.

As a first step in meeting their obligation to reduce the risks of violence to their staff, *employers should issue an authoritative statement of intent*. This will demonstrate to employees that their employer considers violence towards employees and the risk of violence to be serious matters. The statement of intent should be a clear commitment on the employer's part to be fully supportive of staff who have been subjected to violence and to take positive action to minimize potential risks. Within a local education authority, this statement should have the full backing of the elected members, particularly as there may well be resource implications.

The statement of intent should cover the following:

- a commitment on the part of the employer to introduce measures for combating violence to employees;
- a declaration of full support for staff who have been assaulted or suffered verbal abuse, including confirmation that reporting incidents of violence will not be seen as an adverse reflection on the individual's ability to perform their duties satisfactorily;
- appropriate investigation of all reported incidents of violence;
- notification to the police of all assaults on an employee by a manager or other senior member of staff (unless the employee objects);
- provision of legal advice and representation by the employer following incidents in which the police will not prosecute; in appropriate cases, employees can then start proceedings for alleged assault, malicious damage, etc.;
- sending of formal warning letters by the employer to people making threats or verbally abusing staff, where appropriate; the letters should warn that legal action may be taken if a breach of the law occurs;
- arrangements for liaison with employers of contract staff working at the premises.

Plan of action

When planning for safety, the employer and senior managers should:

- consult governors, employees, parents, and where appropriate, pupils and students;
- take into account existing safety procedures, physical danger points and any structural changes needed;
- where there are cost implications, incorporate the plan of action into the establishment's development and budgetary plans.

Written policies and procedures

The school's safety policy should indicate what arrangements are to be set in place for:

- researching and understanding the nature of the problem;
- reporting and recording of incidents and 'near misses';
- developing a preventive strategy;
- understanding the role of the police;
- implementing the measures within the plan of action;
- monitoring and reviewing the effectiveness of measures;
- ensuring all staff, particularly new staff and temporary staff, are made aware of the school's safety policy and procedure;
- providing support for staff involved in incidents.

This matter is more fully dealt with in Chapters 7 and 8.

References

1 Health and Safety Executive (1990), *A Guide to the Health and Safety at Work etc. Act 1974* (4th edn), London: HMSO.
2 Health and Safety Executive (1996), *Reporting of Injuries, Diseases and Dangerous Occurrences Regulations*, London: HSE.
3 Health and Safety Executive (1992), *Management of Health and Safety Regulations 1992 – Approved Code of Practice*, London: HSE Books.
4 Mayhew, P., Elliott, D. and Dowds, L. (1989), *The 1988 British Crime Survey*, Home Office Research Study No. 111, London: HMSO.
5 Health and Safety Executive, op. cit.
6 National Association of Head Teachers (1996), *Managing Risk Assessment*, Professional Management Series, Pamphlet No. PM008, London: NAHT, February.
7 Ibid.
8 Ibid.

6 The principles of risk assessment

Once it has been recognized that both employers and employees have duties in respect of safe working practices, and that failure to combat violence at work has potentially serious costs, many organizations start to take positive steps to tackle the problems. The systematic approach of a risk assessment will help to achieve a coherent policy backed by procedures for implementation.

An assessment of risk is nothing more than a careful examination of what, in the workplace, can cause harm. The primary aim is to work towards creating a policy for the organization on violence and aggression in the workplace as part of its overall health and safety policy.

This is not a once-and-for-all activity; it should be monitored and evaluated. Reviews should form part of standard management practice.

There are no hard and fast rules about how risk assessment should be undertaken. Risk assessment can be summarized as follows:

1 **Look for the hazards** – Decide how this will be done, whether informally, or through a detailed risk assessment audit. Decide what investigation method is most appropriate.
2 **Classify all incidents, as well as 'near misses' and 'nasty moments'** – Decide who might be harmed and how. Consult all staff about details of incidents, including details of intruders, approaches to children outside the school, indecent telephone calls, threatening behaviour and drug/solvent abuse. Keep a record to highlight patterns of activity – establish a database if the organization is large, such as a further education college.
3 **Search for preventive measures** – Evaluate the risks arising from the hazards and decide whether existing precautions are adequate or more should be done.
4 **Create the establishment's safety policy and procedures** – Put measures into practice.

5   **Check that the measures work** – Review your assessment from time to time, and revise it as necessary.

The process should be practical, and should involve governors, senior managers and employees, including union representatives, whether or not advisers or consultants deal with the detail.

Help and advice are available from a number of organizations involved in education: in particular, headteachers' organizations have produced advice on how schools can go about the task of managing their security.

Putting principles into practice

Defining the hazards

The easiest way to determine the hazards is to ask the staff. This can be done informally by managers, supervisors, safety representatives, union representatives, or through a short questionnaire.

- Be systematic, and ensure all relevant risks to personal safety are addressed by setting up an agreed method of investigation.
- Ensure the level of detail in risk assessment is broadly proportionate to the risk. It is not necessary to catalogue every trivial hazard. Nor are employers expected to anticipate hazards beyond the limits of current knowledge.
- Address what *really* happens in the workplace. Actual practice may differ from instructions. Non-routine operations may be overlooked, and need to be taken into account.
- Ensure that all groups of employees who might be affected are considered and consulted.
- Identify employees who may be particularly at risk.
- Take account of existing preventive or precautionary measures – are they working properly? Does action need to be taken to ensure they are maintained?
- Even if no problem is found, it is wise to check the position again from time to time, because the situation may change.
- Record all incidents. By keeping a detailed record of all incidents, a picture of the problem will emerge. A simple report form can be used to obtain the details of what happened, where, when, who was involved, and any possible causes. (A sample incident report form is included in Appendix D.)

As we have already seen, employees may not report incidents for all sorts of reasons. Employees should be encouraged to report *all* incidents, however minor. It is important to impress upon employees that failure to report an incident may put others at risk.

A wide variety of services and jobs are performed in education; the degree of risk faced may vary according to the work carried out. Some examples of these activities and types of staff who may be at risk are given below. This list is by no means complete. Managers will need to look carefully at the tasks carried out by their employees and consider which groups may be at risk. Some staff will carry out a number of activities, and may therefore face risks from more than one source.

Activities	Staff
caretaking, looking after premises and resource areas	caretakers, porters, security staff, laboratory, workshop and resource technicians
working alone	cleaning staff, library staff, headteachers, teachers, gardeners and groundspeople
home visiting	education welfare officers, education social workers, teachers, college outreach workers
evening working	teaching staff, library staff, cleaning staff, education welfare officers, youth and community workers, caretaking staff
running licensed premises in education establishments	campus bar staff
providing food	kitchen staff
looking after animals/ research with animals	animal house technicians, teaching staff, research workers
working with pupils with behavioural difficulties	teachers, educational psychologists, day care helpers, classroom auxiliaries, school counsellors
working with truants and latecomers	educational welfare officers, home tuition teachers, educational charity workers
looking after money	headteachers, school secretaries, clerical staff

supervising pupils/   headteachers, teachers, midday
    disciplining pupils   supervisors

dealing with angry parents   headteachers, teachers, education
    or relatives of pupils   officers, school secretaries,
                                 receptionists

travelling in the course of educational welfare officers, advisers,
    their work   inspectors, external verifiers, outreach
                                 workers, teachers, peripatetic teachers,
                                 teachers of Gypsy children

Classify all incidents

Senior managers will also want to know what kinds of incident are happening, and to whom. This means classifying incidents under various headings – place, time, type of incident, who was involved, and the possible causes.

The National Association of Head Teachers have developed a sensible chart for ranking risks:[1]

Level of risk	Description
Not significant	a risk that is unlikely to result in minor injury or illness leading to lost time, disablement or death
Low	a risk that will improbably result in minor injury or illness leading to lost time, disablement or death
Moderate	a risk that is likely to result in injury or illness leading to lost time, disablement or death
High	a risk that is highly probable, and will result in serious injury or illness leading to lost time, disablement or death
Very high	a risk that will certainly result in serious injury or illness leading to lost time, disablement or death

It should be easy to classify 'major injuries', but it is necessary to decide how to classify 'serious or persistent verbal abuse', not only to cover all incidents that worry staff, but also satisfy the Health and Safety Regulations 1992. This is not easy, because it is a very subjective area. Each individual can react differently to threats or abuse. The seriousness may need to be judged by the effect it has on the recipient.

Details on the incident report form, along with these classifications, can be used to check for patterns. Look for common causes, areas or times. The steps taken can then be targeted where they are most needed.

Account should also be taken of potential incidents when no actual harm has resulted. Staff may have felt considerably frightened, or may have realized how easily the situation could have escalated into a real problem. These experiences may produce an informative pattern when they are taken into account.

Before embarking on any audit, it is important to be clear about the information needed, to establish whether the audit will deal with one or more departments, and whether it is aimed at particular groups of staff or employees who undertake particular tasks. It is helpful to collect information about staff feelings and attitudes to the problem of violence at work, and about the level of awareness of staff in relation to safety procedures. Information will also be needed about actual incidents of violence.

Classification methods

Some investigation methods involve the collection of 'hard' data – yes/no answers, numerical scores, choices from a checklist, etc. Examples include the number of incidents of violence, the percentage of people feeling at risk, or rankings of what staff believe are the most dangerous situations. This sort of data is easy to collate and quantify.

Other methods generate information which is more difficult to quantify, but which can be helpful in forming a picture of staff views, opinions and anecdotal evidence. Descriptions of procedures used, and individual views about how these might be improved, fall within this category.

The simpler the information to be collected, the easier it will be to use. The key is to achieve a balance between simplicity and the collection of useful information. Senior managers should remember that large quantities of information may be difficult to handle effectively, and that resources will be needed to analyse and present the audit findings. It is important at the outset to commit sufficient resources to handle the audit, and to set a realistic time scale for the exercise. A simple, straightforward approach generates information that can be readily analysed and acted upon. It is well worth making time at the planning stage to do the groundwork thoroughly, as this will increase the chances of getting exactly what is needed from the investigation, in a form that is manageable and will actually save time in the long run.

Methods of collecting information include the use of questionnaires, observation, structured interviews, working groups and the use of external consultants. Other methods which have proved effective include:

- suggestion boxes;
- meetings attended by senior managers, heads of departments or faculties, ancillary supervisors or managers;
- staff meetings or departmental meetings;
- asking people to write in with views, ideas, problems, opinions, etc.;

- open forums with safety or personnel staff;
- visits to other workplaces to observe different practices.

It is necessary to remember that no method is perfect, nor will it give precisely all the information sought. Whichever method or combination of methods is selected, people should be made aware of what is being done and why, and involved whenever possible. The outcome of the audit exercise should also be made available as quickly as possible.

The organization may have staff with skills and experience in information collection and management. If it does not, or if staff are already fully stretched, then it may be necessary to seek external help in conducting an audit. Such a decision may reduce staff anxiety and encourage honesty and openness; management may also be more accepting of an external view of the findings.

Where the decision is to conduct the audit 'in-house', an existing or specially created joint management–staff group can be given the task of conducting the investigation. This is often regarded as the best option to secure contributions, co-operation and commitment to the process and its outcomes.

Search for preventive measures

Having evaluated the risks arising from the hazards, it is necessary to decide whether the precautions are already adequate or more needs to be done. There are no ready-made remedies. The employer (and senior managers) will have to find measures that are right for their particular establishment. Even such matters as how teaching is organized and how the school day is designed have a bearing upon matters of safety.

A mix of measures will often work best. It is important to balance the risks to employees against any possible side effects to visiting parents. An atmosphere that suggests employees are worried about violence can sometimes increase its likelihood.

Finally, the findings should be acted upon as soon as practicable. There may well be risks which can be dealt with immediately, and these should be tackled, thus reassuring staff of the commitment to act. Other more complex problems may take time to deal with; where this is the case, it is important to keep staff in touch with progress that is being made, so that they know the problem is being tackled.

References

1   National Association of Head Teachers (1996), *Managing Risk Assessment*, Professional Management Series, Pamphlet No. PM008, London: NAHT, February.

7 Developing a policy

As stated earlier, the best way to respond to those obligations which the Health and Safety at Work Act places on employers and employees is to develop a formal, written policy. Most schools will already have a health and safety policy written out in general terms. However, this may need to be reworked to comply with the health and safety regulations on the personal safety issue.

In this context, a policy is a document that sets out the course of action to be pursued by the organization (both employers and employees) in order to fulfil its obligations in law and in respect of national or workplace agreements.

A policy provides a framework on which procedures and practices can be built. It makes it possible to require or demand appropriate behaviour or action in relation to safety matters. Furthermore, a policy provides clarity, demonstrates commitment and develops confidence in the organization's willingness to address the issue of violence at work. While the responsibility for policy is a managerial one, the usual – and generally most effective – process for developing policy is a joint one, where management and staff negotiate and agree it.

Developing any policy, especially where meeting its requirements can have a cost to the organization (in financial, resource or time terms) or to the individual (in terms of demands on them, required behaviour, changes in practice) can be fraught with difficulty. The management and staff roles in negotiating it can become adversarial and time-consuming. The consultative process can be extremely protracted. Worst of all, the policy can end up so watered down in rendering it acceptable to all that it does not achieve its purpose. Having said all that, a policy that is not jointly developed, negotiated and agreed is unlikely to be 'owned' by people generally, so it may not have their commitment or confidence.

Before starting the process of developing the policy, it is helpful to be clear about who needs to be involved in the development process, and how. Thought should be given as to whether those involved should be senior management, staff representatives, administrative and reception staff, and specialist staff. Their powers and remit will need to be agreed, and decisions will need to be made about who should be party to agreements, including governors and managers, union representatives, other staff representatives and representatives of non-union staff.

Agreement will need to be reached on the timescale for the development, the consultation process and finalization of the policy. This will depend to a large extent on the resources and support that will be required throughout the process, and the limited availability of busy people, which can slow the process considerably. Being clear about the priority given to this task and planning meeting dates will help the group to keep to the timescale. The tasks may not be straightforward or easy, and people who commit themselves to assisting in the process should understand what their commitment entails.

Those involved will need to realize that the agreed policy may mean changes or costs that people will wish to resist. Management and the development group need to be very clear about the extent to which they must take views into account and the extent to which they may impose their own.

The policy document

The following areas would normally be covered by a policy on violence at work.

Policy title

The policy title needs to make it clear what the policy is about in general terms. Examples of titles include: 'Combating Violence at Work'; 'XYZ Trust Policy on Violence to Staff'; 'Safety from Violence at Work – a Policy Statement'; 'Health and Safety Policy – Violence to Staff'.

If the policy on violence to staff is part of an overall health and safety policy, it ought to be identifiable within the main policy, and an explicit title can help in this.

The purpose

This should be a general statement of what the policy is intended to achieve. It does not need to go into any detail. For example, the purpose could be described as follows:

- to reduce the risks to staff from violence;
- to fulfil legal and other obligations by ensuring the safety of staff;
- to protect staff from all forms of violence whenever possible, and to provide after-care should staff be subjected to violence;
- to ensure that everyone in the organization is aware of and fulfils their responsibility for safety from violence at work.

Definition

This should set out what the organization and this particular policy means by 'violence at work'. It should indicate what behaviour and actions are included and excluded from the definition of 'violence' used (see Chapter 4).

The philosophy

This section describes the basis from which the policy starts – the values and beliefs underlying it that can be expressed as a series of statements, for example:

- All violence to staff is unacceptable, whatever form it takes and whatever reasons are cited for it.
- We recognize the risks to staff from violence at work and the obligations of the organization to minimize the risks.
- Dealing with, or being subject to, violent behaviour is not considered to be a failure on the part of an employee.
- Violence is not considered to be an acceptable part of any job, nor is it part of the duties of any employee to accept violent behaviour.
- We recognize the potentially damaging effects of violence on individuals, work performance and the organization as a whole, and are committed to combating it.

Whom the policy covers

All staff in the organization may be subject to the policy and its requirements, or it may be a policy developed for a particular site, department or group of staff with a unique role in the organization.

It is also important to be clear about whether the policy applies to permanent staff only, or also to temporary staff and others who may be working in the organization for a short time.

What the employer is committed to do

Examples of the actions that the employer will take include:

- analysis/audit within the organization to identify risks, hazards, problems or other issues;
- preventive measures to combat the risks of violence at work, such as changes in the environment, procedures and practices;
- data collection or monitoring of incidents of violence to staff, and actions as a result of the information gathered;
- communication of the policy to ensure that everyone is aware of it and their responsibility with respect to it;
- allocation of specific roles and responsibilities in support of the policy, such as: assigning a manager with overall responsibility for the policy; responsibility for monitoring incidents; responsibility for ensuring appropriate after-care for staff who experience violence; responsibility for safety training;
- sanctions to be taken in the event of violent behaviour by an employee of the organization;
- formal, written warning to be given to any individual who has made threats of violence towards an employee; this warning should indicate that legal action may be taken if there is a breach of the law;
- after-care procedures to be made available, such as: counselling, time off work, earnings protection, help in bringing a court case, assistance with compensation claims or medical assistance;
- evaluation and review of the policy and procedures at agreed intervals, and the continual development of practice;
- putting in place an appropriate joint management–staff forum, with a health and safety remit or a specific remit in relation to violence at work;
- training of staff to ensure that they can fulfil their responsibilities under the policy and protect themselves from violence at work; this should also cover the issue of restraint in special residential or day care settings.

What is required of individuals

This section could contain a general statement outlining the obligation of employees to take reasonable care of themselves and other people who may be affected by their acts or omissions. Other areas this section could cover include:

- the requirement to operate procedures as laid down, such as entry procedures, wearing of badges, notification to reception of visitors expected, booking in and out of the workplace, use of a diary system, and so on;
- attendance at training events, such as those concerned with the policy,

the implementation of procedures, systems such as reporting of incidents of violence or more specialist events for managers, special needs staff, travelling staff or other groups;

- reporting of incidents of violence, using the procedures available to them;
- the particular roles of individuals, for example supervisors, senior managers (such as heads of department), chief administrative officers, caretakers, teaching and non-teaching personnel, safety and welfare staff, and those responsible for staff development/training;
- reporting of hazards, risks or problems that individuals identify or become aware of in the course of their work.

Performance measures

The inclusion of performance measures within the policy means that the effectiveness of the policy can be assessed in relation to them. Performance measures may include:

- a reduction in the number of incidents, over a given period;
- a nil return, within a given period, of assaults on staff;
- a reduction in the proportion of staff who are verbally abused in a given period or a particular area of work;
- a reduction in the number of working days lost as a consequence of incidents of violence or aggression;
- fewer staff feeling concerned or afraid of violence and aggression at work, or a raised level of morale (this may require a survey or other analysis before and after the implementation of the policy, so that comparisons can be made);
- a reduction in the rate of increase in incidents of violence or threats to staff;
- fewer staff leaving because of fears of aggressive behaviour, fear of violence or actual violence (exit interviews are one way of gathering this information);
- reductions in compensation claims or payments, or insurance premiums.

Performance measures can be developed for the whole organization, parts of it, or specific types of work. They are particularly useful in assessing the effectiveness of newly-developed procedures. Performance measures that can help to demonstrate such effects as fewer working days lost, higher morale, greater productivity or lower turnover of staff assist in justifying the costs of security equipment, changing procedures or other measures taken to make the workplace safer.

Evaluation/review

The policy itself should include information about how its effectiveness will be assessed. It could give details of who will take responsibility, when assessment will take place, the process that will be used, and how the results will be communicated to people and acted on.

Similar methods to those used in investigating the risks of violence at work (see Chapter 6) can be used in evaluation, including questionnaires, group meetings, observation and structured interviews.

An evaluation process based directly on assessment against performance measures within the policy can be developed. Evaluation data can also be obtained from data generated by other systems, such as personnel systems – for example, staff turnover figures, exit interview reports, or fewer problems in recruiting staff.

In addition, when a violence at work incident-reporting system is in place, this will provide direct data on the scale of the problem and any changes in it, including an increase or decrease in people seeking some sort of after-care.

Finally, in developing a new policy, it is wise to incorporate the first review date into the policy to ensure that a review does take place. Thereafter, reviews should be conducted at regular intervals, but may not need to be very frequent.

Resource implications

It is clear that a properly organized system to ensure the personal safety of employees will involve some costs. Measures for dealing with violent incidents, and for providing after-care and support to those involved, all have resource implications. Employers will need to examine the cost implications of those procedures which can contribute to, or reduce, the risk of violence towards staff.

Staff working late will need to be reviewed to check whether these patterns of work are really necessary. Staffing levels may need re-appraisal, so that there is the capacity to provide additional support in potentially violent situations, for example by making arrangements for joint home visits by educational welfare officers.

The provision of counselling where individuals have experienced violence is also likely to involve re-allocation of staff time, and the services of a paid counsellor from within or outside the establishment.

Developing an effective personal safety strategy, and preparing and supporting staff to play their part, will involve awareness-raising and training for staff at all levels. The introduction of personal safety training as part of an organization's personal safety strategy cannot be achieved without the commitment of additional resources. Rather than being seen as yet another area to be added to a long list of training needs, it is helpful to recognize that personal safety underpins good practice in many other areas. Effective use of scarce resources will be enhanced where the employees are confident and well supported, and where opportunities for violent or aggressive behaviour are kept to a minimum.

All parts of the education sector face spending constraints and may not relish yet further demands on scarce resources. Nevertheless, employers have a clear legal and moral duty to secure the safety of their staff and to reduce the chances of compensation claims arising. Additional resources will need to be found in order to provide a safe working environment.

8 Implementing policy – developing procedures

Developing and agreeing a policy is a vital step towards a coherent organizational response to violence at work, but it is only one step. Policies often stop at the point where they are statements of intent, and while the intentions are good, little action follows because of the lack of procedures.

The policy itself says *what* people will do; the procedures then go on to say *how* they will do things. The procedures required will depend on what the policy says, the nature and scale of the problem faced by the organization, and the nature of the organization itself in terms of size, culture and its educational work. The procedures that may need to be stipulated include:

- how particular jobs or tasks should be performed, for example:

    - reception duties;
    - interviewing parents;
    - securing the premises;

- working practices, such as:

    - notification of names and number of visitors; signing in and out;
    - wearing of identification badges;
    - controlling access to buildings or parts of them;

- working patterns, for example:

    - working away from the main place of work and the use of diary sheets, signing-in and signing-out systems;
    - security procedures when working late;
    - working in other people's homes or premises;
    - travelling in the line of duty;

- how to obtain and use security equipment, such as:

- mobile telephones/car telephones;
- personal alarms;
- two-way radios;

- tradespeople, contractors and deliveries:

  - a nominated contact person in charge of people working on the premises;
  - checks or vetting of people who will work temporarily on the premises;
  - reception of people into the organization, and systems for identifying them while they are working;

- how to provide training in support of the policy, such as:

  - induction for new staff;
  - general health and safety;
  - relaxation and tension control;
  - communication skills;
  - interpersonal skills;
  - assertiveness training;
  - how to operate procedures;
  - practical techniques for protection;
  - specialist training, e.g. counselling;
  - managers' roles in policy implementation;

- how to monitor incidents of violence, including:

  - a reporting system;
  - a report form;
  - a nominated member of staff responsible for reports and monitoring information;
  - the use of monitoring information;

- how to follow up incidents of violence and provide after-care, for example:

  - actions the organization will take to assist teaching and non-teaching staff who are subjected to violence directly, such as time off work, protected earnings;
  - services the organization will obtain, e.g. counselling;
  - support available for staff who have been assaulted or threatened, e.g. legal advice, medical assistance;
  - compensation for damage to property or for injuries suffered;

- routine safety checking, such as:

  - locking up, nominated keyholders, setting alarms;

- – testing of safety equipment;
- – maintenance and repair of safety equipment or systems;
- – reporting faults or risks to people responsible for safety precautions;

- procedures for evaluation/review of the policy, including:

- – when they will take place;
- – who is responsible for evaluation and review, and how it will be done;
- – how the results will be communicated.

The procedures should set out in detail the agreed view of how the establishment should respond after an act of violence or aggression. Any action should balance the need to avoid condoning violence with the need to avoid precipitating any further incident. Priority must be given to preventing a recurrence and assisting the affected person.

9 Reporting violent incidents

Effective reporting and monitoring of incidents are identified by Poyner and Warne as the single most important factor in attempting to make workplaces and staff safer.[1]

A formal system for reporting and recording incidents will be needed to:

- devise appropriate preventive strategies;
- monitor whether these strategies are effective.

Staff will need to be positively encouraged to report incidents, if a true picture of their nature and frequency is to be built up.

Good in-house reporting and recording systems are essential in order to identify places, groups and activities where violence can be a problem. A report form needs to contain sufficient detail to help identify appropriate preventive measures, and to help assess whether those measures were successful. Suggested details include information on:

- where the incident occurred, including physical environment; the time of day;
- activity at the time of the incident:
- details of the perpetrator;
- the relationship between victim and perpetrator;
- an account of what happened;
- the outcome;
- if preventing measures have been introduced, were they of help?

Senior staff commitment

People with responsibility for staff management need to be committed to the objective of reducing risk of violence and threats of violence to employees. Any member of staff at any level is at risk. The Education Service Advisory Committee strongly recommends that all staff receive appropriate training before the policy and procedures are introduced. Training should cover:

- understanding the definition of 'violence' and how violence can develop;
- understanding the effect that a perceived risk as well as a real risk can have on staff morale and stress levels;
- clarification of the staff role in implementing the employer's preventive strategy;
- being supportive of staff who have been victims of violence;
- knowing what action to take when a violent incident has occurred.

The problem of under-reporting

The under-reporting of violent incidents is a significant factor in monitoring such attacks and in developing responses, and its importance cannot be overemphasized. Unless there are accurate records, it is difficult to make a case for the allocation of additional resources to develop a safety strategy.

There are a number of reasons why people fail to report violence or threats of violence. Some staff find it particularly difficult to report or discuss incidents of verbal abuse or threats, for fear that it may reflect on their professional ability to manage classes, or damage their prospects for promotion. People working in caring professions, such as education, are notoriously reluctant to ask for help from others; their work is stressful, however, and it is all too easy for insecure staff to tolerate negative or threatening behaviour.

In some areas, the local political climate may encourage a culture of problem-denial, with staff feeling under pressure not to report incidents which they feel reflect adversely on them or on their employing establishment. Fearing accusations of prejudice, or contravention of expected standards, senior personnel may deal with certain offenders with inappropriate leniency.

There is also a tendency for people to assume that women are more at risk than men. Not only does this run counter to all the statistical evidence available (with the exception of domestic violence), but this attitude places pressure upon men to deny feelings of vulnerability.

The same could be said of senior managers. The accepted view is that an inexperienced employee is likely to be more vulnerable than experienced, more senior members of staff. In fact, it is often the case that headteachers, their deputies and year heads place themselves at risk every day when attempting to expel intruders or to calm angry parents.

On the other hand, some staff have said that they have experienced, or feared, unhelpful responses from management, including blaming the victim, failing to recognize the seriousness of the situation, and suggesting that they had over-reacted in some way. Indeed, it is fair to say that some institutions have, in the past, failed to take seriously the experiences and concerns of staff facing aggression, in case the acknowledgement of such incidents should damage the establishment's reputation. Today's competitive climate has made establishments even more concerned to present a trouble-free image.

These findings highlight the need for governors and employers to accept responsibility for preventing and responding to violence in a positive and staff-supportive manner. Once again, it is a question of encouraging a climate of change, so that all staff feel that reporting will not reflect on their ability to do a particular job. Safety awareness training, and training on making effective use of agreed procedures and guidelines, should be routine for all governors and managers in educational establishments.

Everyone working in the field of education has a responsibility to themselves and their colleagues to help prevent violent incidents. Part of this responsibility involves the reporting of any incidents which do occur. People need to be assured that it is not a sign of personal or professional failure to be attacked or threatened, and reminded that under-reporting or secrecy can expose them and other staff to serious risks. Information about incidents will also help in the development of effective strategies for preventing violence, and will help in the design of personal safety training programmes.

Reporting systems

Where they already exist, reporting systems can themselves form part of an investigation of risks at work, or they may be developed after a risk assessment audit as part of the procedures for implementing policy.

Some organizations use existing accident report systems to record incidents of violence. There are drawbacks to this approach, however. Accident reports are not generally filed unless actual injury results from the incident, so their use can give a false picture of the level of violent incidents and lead to a false sense of security. The use of accident report forms contributes to a perception that only incidents where someone has suffered an injury or financial loss should be reported. It often does not register that there is an equal and important need to record threats, racial abuse and other forms of harassment.

A separate system using a form to record violent incidents or 'near misses' usually works best. A simple form that can be completed by, or on behalf of, someone subjected to violence provides information that can be analysed and used in the development of future preventive measures. Useful information to collect on the form includes:

- time, day and date of the incident, as this may help identify periods of risk, patterns of incidents at certain times, or people at risk because of the times they work;
- a sketch or description of the location of the incident can sometimes help identify design flaws which contribute to risk that can be rectified;
- an account of what happened leading up to and during the incident can, for example, highlight a need for back-up staff; indicate where normal practice leaves staff vulnerable; suggest that alarms or panic button systems are required or that training is needed to help staff operate existing procedures or develop skills in managing aggressive people;
- attempting to identify causes and motives may help to suggest where systems and procedures may trigger violence, or extreme or aggressive behaviours, for example

  - when people have been kept waiting;
  - when people cannot get access to someone they believe can help;
  - when documentation or letters are not understood;

- the name and details of the employee attacked, although it may be decided that forms can be completed anonymously.

Once a form has been designed, it is best to start using it to gauge how well it works. It may be necessary to redesign the form in the light of early experience of its use. The record of assessment form suggested by the Education Service Advisory Committee can be found in Appendix C and the Health and Safety Executive's incident report form on violence and aggression to staff is in Appendix D.

As the report of the incident is not the end of the matter, it is sensible to keep records of the effects of the incident on the worker and property, as well as details of follow-up actions taken and after-care for the staff member. This information can be kept separately or on the reverse of the incident report form and completed by the nominated person responsible.

The incident report form must remain confidential; people will not feel inclined to report incidents unless they feel sure that their privacy will be protected. Monitoring information or details for management reports can still be extracted from incident report forms without identifying the staff members concerned.

It is essential that all employees are aware of the procedures for reporting violent incidents. They will need to know who has overall responsibility for the procedure and how to obtain an incident report form. Guidance about how the form should be completed should be provided, together with information about where to get help if this is needed, and what should be done with the completed form.

Information should also be provided to all staff, especially non-teaching staff, about whom they should go to for advice, help and support or for any of the after-care services, and how they will receive information about any follow-up action taken when an incident has been reported.

References

1 Poyner, B. and Warne, C. (1986), *Violence to Staff – A Basis for Assessment and Prevention*, London: HMSO.

Part 3

Reducing the risks

10 The workplace

This chapter contains a series of guidelines on good practice in relation to personal safety for those in the education sector while they are at work. Education settings vary tremendously in their size and their complexity: the larger the site and the greater the number of buildings, the higher the likely cost of securing the premises. Although the outcomes of any attempt to 'design out' risk will vary according to the budget (for example, the average-sized primary school is unlikely to consider installing closed-circuit TV), nevertheless, the principles which underpin the suggestions made in this chapter are the same regardless of the type and size of establishment. In many cases, solutions to problems of security can be simple and low-cost.

The Elton Report made some recommendations about school premises which can help to improve and maintain the quality of a school's environment, for example:

- arrangements should be made for the immediate repair of minor damage and the removal of graffiti;
- those with responsibility for buildings should ensure that school buildings are designed with durability (consistent with attractiveness), ease of maintenance, avoidance of circulation bottlenecks and good sight-lines for the supervision of pupils in mind;
- the government, in its expenditure plans, should give explicit encouragement to LEAs and governing bodies with responsibility for buildings to ensure that adequate funds are made available for the maintenance of school premises.[1]

More useful information and ideas on security and design improvements to reduce vulnerability to intruders is contained in *Building Bulletin 67: Crime Prevention in Schools*, published by the Department of Education and Science

(DES) in 1987,[2] and other guidance on the security of school premises is available from the Department for Education and Employment (DfEE).

The environs

Employers and employees will be well aware that the environs of the workplace – the grounds, gardens and parking areas – are still part of the premises, and need to be looked at from the point of view of safety. Even where the surrounding areas are not part of the employer's premises, employee safety in these areas should still be considered: after all, they are only there because this is their place of work.

Visibility is an important issue in grounds and car parks: people need to be able to see and be seen. Proper lighting is an essential part of ensuring visibility, but it will only be of limited use if people are obscured by walls, fencing or vegetation. It may be necessary to consider opening up areas by removing walls and fences and keeping hedges and bushes pruned. Where the employer does not own the car park used by employees, then representation should be made to the owners so that it can be made safer. If car parks are multi-storey, as in certain local authority buildings or university campuses, they need to be well-lit throughout, particularly in stairways.

Sometimes, protecting the grounds and car parks of a workplace with fencing or walls is feasible and worthwhile. An entry card system can be used, with gates or barriers to allow employees' vehicles through, or there can be a control operated by security staff.

In large establishments, closed-circuit TV surveillance of grounds and car parks is now more common. It enables security or other designated staff to see what is happening outside from a safe position. Bleepers, mobile phones and walkie-talkies can be invaluable in ensuring that any incident can be reported immediately and/or the security staff can go to the aid of someone in difficulty.

Thought should be given to items left around in car parks or grounds: all sorts of everyday items are potential weapons. Some, such as gardening tools, are very dangerous when misused. Pebbles, loose or detachable stones and paving slabs can be used as missiles.

Sensor-activated additional lighting can be useful to give light to those re-entering the premises in the evening or to alert security staff or others that an unknown person is present and that something may be wrong. External alarm points known to staff could be activated if help were needed. Emergency lighting is useful in case of power failure.

Access to the workplace

Although difficulties are presented by some schools such as the post-war primary schools, the general design and physical environment of the buildings can sometimes be improved in order to reduce the likelihood of violence. For instance, it is vital in today's climate to consider the access route to a school or college. There may be many entrances, although the main route for the public will probably be through the reception area. Certainly, this area is important. However, most schools and colleges have back doors, fire doors, service bays, car park entrances, playing fields, yards, and so on. All these are potential points of access into the building, and may well be preferred points of access for anyone with criminal activity in mind.

Even where there is general public access to a building, it is possible to confine that access to public areas, so that employees come to meet the public, rather than finding members of the public wandering around the building. Limiting access can be achieved by using:

- locked doors that can be operated by a key, a key card or access number punched in by staff;
- one-way doors – these can be used by staff and students to exit at any time and meet fire regulations, but entry can only be effected by use of a key system;
- offices near the reception or waiting area where employees can meet members of the public and can see and be seen by reception staff or other staff on duty.

Access to buildings (where there is no general public access) or to parts of buildings can also be controlled if:

- all visitors and other callers are notified to reception or security to ensure they are expected;
- visitors and/or tradespersons use the entrance marked;
- visitors sign in and out, so it is known who is in the building and when they leave;
- all legitimate visitors wear a pass or visitor's badge;
- all visitors are met by an employee, and remain their responsibility throughout the visit;
- 'no entry' signs are installed;
- 'staff only' notices are posted;
- in large establishments and multi-campus establishments such as further education colleges, staff wear identity badges so they are clearly identified as staff;

- there is a reception or security area in each building, where schools and colleges occupy more than one;
- all tradespeople, contractors and deliveries have a named employee contact who is aware of their business and supervises them while on the premises, and ensures that:
    - they have appointments;
    - they are checked in;
    - their credentials are checked;
    - there are practice guidelines for them: where they can go, what they can do, required standards of behaviour, and sanctions in the contract;
    - they are checked out.

Many schools and colleges have multiple points of access and operate an open-access policy for pupils and their families and friends. Whilst this policy undoubtedly assists home–school co-operation, it has left pupils and staff vulnerable to attack by intruders. A managed access policy will work towards maintaining a balance between keeping access as open as possible while taking steps to reduce the opportunities for intrusion.

Dealing with access points other than main doors can be a problem. It is often difficult to persuade staff and pupils to keep back doors and side entrances locked. It is not unusual to find one-way fire doors propped open for the convenience of staff. Apart from breaking fire regulations, this leaves the building vulnerable. Delivery or loading bays and vehicle and service entrances are also potential access points that people rarely think of controlling from the point of view of staff safety.

Managers need to continue to insist that fire doors are kept shut at all times; they should not be used as normal exits unless this is unavoidable. All other side doors, rear doors, doors to car parks or garages can be self-closing/self-locking doors, or they can be self-closing one-way doors, like fire doors. Staff may need to be provided with keys or key cards, or they may have to learn an entry code if such a system is used.

Delivery or loading bays, vehicle entrances and service entrances are sometimes more difficult to deal with directly. What has proved successful for some establishments is to isolate these areas from the rest of the workplace. Thus, rather than controlling access to them, access from them into other areas of the workplace is controlled by the use of locked doors. Access to these areas can also be controlled by using fences or otherwise enclosing them, if possible. Premises should therefore have entrances with clear, unambiguous signs, which may need to be repeated at intervals.

Reception areas/waiting rooms

Most education establishments have reception systems which help reduce the numbers of visitors wandering around the premises. The reception area should preferably be located close to the premises' main entrance, easily identifiable and accessible. This is the area where the majority of people will start their contact with the organization. If someone has come to sort out a disagreement, deal with a problem, make a complaint or is there other than by choice, the effect of a good reception system could be quite significant. The way in which people are received when they arrive is likely to increase or reduce feelings of anger or distress.

Evidence from research shows that colour can affect mood and perception. Dark, dingy places feel different from bright, welcoming, warm ones. Institutional colours, such as grey and greens, can lead to certain perceptions of places, or confirm our prejudices of what places (and possibly the people in them, too) are like. Being left to wait in a dark, dingy, cold or grubby room is unlikely to improve anyone's mood. A bright, warm, comfortable setting will not guarantee good humour, but it is likely to be calming rather than irritating.

Just as the environment can affect people coming into it as visitors, it can also affect the people who work there, even to the point of predisposing them to behaviour that may elicit an aggressive response. A number of organizations have taken this research seriously and applied it to reception and waiting areas in the following ways:

- using pastel colours;
- putting flowers or plants in waiting areas;
- using light and airy rooms for waiting;
- providing comfortable, robust furniture;
- making reading material available;
- ensuring there are toilet facilities;
- when possible, making sure there is adequate and accessible parking so people do not arrive frustrated, or warning them in advance that they may have difficulty parking.

Organizations that take these sorts of steps believe they are cost-effective and make a difference because:

- difficulty in finding the place, parking and so on is minimized, and so is frustration;
- people feel welcome and expected;
- it appears that the education establishment has respect for visitors and concern for their comfort;

- people are less likely to feel anonymous;
- if people arrive early for their appointment, waiting is relatively pleasurable, so they do not become increasingly uncomfortable, tense and irritated;
- providing books, reading material, refreshments and so on creates diversion and interest and prevents boredom;
- the area can also be used as a positive showcase for students' work.

Reception staff themselves can be in very vulnerable positions, especially where open access means anyone can walk into the premises. Simple, cost-effective measures to reduce the risk to reception staff in smaller education establishments might include:

- reorganizing office layout so that reception staff are visible to other staff;
- making sure reception staff have an escape route should they need it;
- providing a panic button or other alarm system;
- ensuring that under no circumstances is a receptionist, or any other member of staff, left alone in a building which is open to the public.

Among measures taken to protect reception staff in larger establishments, particularly those in high-risk areas, the following have been found to be effective:

- using wider counters, so staff cannot be reached across them;
- installing safety glass screens;
- providing security cameras so that reception staff can see all areas from a safe position;
- providing entry 'phone/entry camera systems in premises with limited access;
- locking access to counter-protected reception areas;
- installing one-way doors in reception areas;
- providing intercom links, to call on back-up from nominated staff, so that colleagues can listen in if they see worrying behaviour.

Undoubtedly, the establishments which have set these measures in place have deemed them necessary, although it should be remembered that what is intended to serve as protection for staff can seem like a barrier to parents and the public. Counters, screens and other devices can trigger aggression or violence in some people when they are perceived as a barrier or block. A balance needs to be struck between creating a welcoming, calming, unthreatening environment for clients and customers and ensuring the safety of staff. Where that balance lies in any given situation will need to be worked out.

Interviewing safely in the workplace

Interviewing, or conducting similar meetings with people, is a task that many employees in all sorts of organizations perform in the course of their work. There have been unfortunate incidents of aggressive and violent behaviour in interviews in many different work settings. Good practice guidelines for interviewing have been derived from a wide range of experience in different work situations, including social services departments, estate agents' offices, social security offices and police stations:

- Make sure that the interview or consultation is not conducted in isolation. Someone needs to know where you are. If possible, use a room in which you are visible to others but not easily overheard, so you can protect confidentiality.
- Make sure that someone knows exactly who you are seeing – and make sure the person knows that their presence is a matter of record.
- It may not be possible to telephone for help, and installing an alarm or panic button should be considered. An alarm with a flashing light can be less disturbing to the whole school, and can avoid creating panic.
- Make sure the room is well-lit but not glaring. Emergency lights may be needed, too.
- Stay near the door – if possible, the room should have two doors.
- All sorts of everyday equipment can provide potential weapons, so keep equipment to the absolute essentials.
- Ensure that furniture is comfortable, but robust enough not to be thrown.
- At the first sign that you are in difficulty (because people can see or hear you, or you have raised the alarm), staff must know who should respond and how, and take immediate action. They should also know who will respond should there be an absentee.
- Do not arrange to meet anyone when you will be alone in the building.
- Prevent waiting time before an interview, where possible.
- If there is waiting time, make sure the visitor knows when they are likely to be seen, and keep them informed.

More detailed guidance on interviewing techniques is included in Chapter 13.

Case conferences

Case conferences provide opportunities for a number of agencies to share information about a particular pupil or family, and to recommend what further action, if any, should be taken. They are an essential ingredient, for example, of child protection work, and increasingly, the parents of the child concerned are invited to attend at least part of the case conference.

Parents are likely to be anxious when called on to discuss the care plan for their child with a group of professionals. They will find the case conference extremely daunting unless they are properly prepared and clear about their own role. Every effort should be made to help them relax and play a positive part in the proceedings.

Parents should be informed in advance of the purpose of the case conference, so that they are prepared psychologically; this will help to avoid surprise and hostile responses at the case conference.

Arrangements for the notification of case conferences, and arrangements for their conduct and administration, should take account of any possible hostile reaction to the sensitive issues which are likely to be discussed. For example, the parents should not be invited too early for the case conference, and should not be kept waiting for a long time once they have arrived. A waiting area should be arranged for the parents, separate from that used by other case conference participants, to avoid unintended pre-case conference discussions. It is important that all the professionals attending case conferences arrive on time.

Pooling of information

Some students or relatives of students will be known from previous experience to be potentially violent or to have displayed aggressive tendencies. For example, it may be known to youth workers that a young person attending a youth centre is aggressive, or perhaps comes from a background where there is a history of family violence. There are occasions when sharing relevant information between sections or between departments can be important in helping to prevent the risk of violence to others. This is a sensitive area, however: the questions of confidentiality and the avoidance of 'labelling' will need to be worked through carefully and fully with the relevant professionals.

Restrictions on disclosure of information on school pupils, as set out in the Education (School Records) Regulations 1989, must be observed.

Handling money or valuables

Staff are sometimes responsible for handling cash. If this becomes generally known, there can be a risk of assault on employees by people who are outside the premises. Most education establishments reduce the handling of cash as far as possible in order to reduce the risk of theft and violence.

In circumstances where cash is collected, it should be banked regularly – preferably collected by security van – making it far less worthwhile for a thief to attempt theft. Staff should know exactly what to do if there is violence in relation to money. Guidelines should be provided, making it quite clear that the first priority is the safety of staff, rather than the safeguarding of money or other valuables. Alarm systems may also be used, so that help can be summoned without the attacker being aware that this is happening.

Storing money and valuables

Where money or valuables are stored as part of the business – for example, in banks or building societies – there are usually very sophisticated forms of security. In premises where money or valuables are only held irregularly, at certain times or for certain purposes, the security is often less well organized. Most offices in educational establishments have a petty cash system which involves the storage of cash for day-to-day expenses and emergency payments, and access and control may be handled in a somewhat casual manner.

Where money is stored on the premises, it is worth considering whether this is strictly necessary. If cash storage can be avoided, it should be. This may involve regular dispatches to the bank. Use the following guidance to avoid the risk of theft and violence:

- Money collected should be taken to the bank each day, rather than being stored.
- Use should be made of a safe and whatever security measures the circumstances demand, such as alarms, cameras, screens, etc.
- Security measures should be obvious.
- Employers should make sure, by providing guidelines, that employees know what to do to protect themselves if the need arises.
- Restrict and control access to the premises, or that part of it where money or valuables are kept.
- Avoid developing a regular pattern of storing money, for example when wages are to be paid.
- Where money or other valuables are stored regularly, seeking specialist security advice is worthwhile. This needs to deal with both the practical security measures and the safety of employees.

Moving money

Where employees do move money themselves, perhaps from the school to the bank, specialist advice can be obtained from security firms or from the police on the particular situation and the risks inherent in it. When using employees to move money, employers should provide guidelines for staff so that they know what to do to protect themselves, making sure they are quite clear that this is their first duty, *not* to protect the money. Staff carrying money should not do so alone.

It is important to avoid establishing a pattern for the movement of money. The day of the week and time of day should vary, as should the route and means of transport, wherever possible. If a number of different people take on this task, this can avoid a specific individual becoming a target for attack.

Some simple, practical steps will also help to reduce the likelihood of attack and robbery. For example:

- Provide people with a means of contact such as a mobile 'phone or two-way radio – this ensures they can keep in touch, raise an alarm or summon help.
- Let the bank or other premises to which they are going know they are on the way and when to expect them – they can then raise the alarm if necessary.
- Use a call-back system, so that the workplace is notified on their safe arrival.
- Consider how money or valuables would best be carried – if a briefcase or bag is carried, it can be snatched; however, if it is attached to an employee, it may be safe from a snatch thief, but this could result in the employee being injured by someone attempting to take it.
- Provide personal attack alarms – they are useful, but only if carried ready for use and used properly, bringing the alarm up sharply and setting it off by the assailant's ear to shock and disorientate them for long enough to walk away quickly, without looking back.
- Ensure that as few people as possible know when, how and by whom money is moved.
- Ensure people are clear about how to proceed in the event of an approach or attack – guidelines should stress that staff should protect themselves, rather than the money they are carrying.

Patterns of work

In many education settings, working late or during the early morning is part of the normal working pattern; in other situations, such as working in a relatively empty building in the school holidays, such arrangements occur on a less regular basis. Whatever patterns apply, good practice takes account of the following:

- technical staff who work during vacations when schools are empty and cleaning staff who work in buildings remote from the main occupied areas and/or work at night, may often be alone and vulnerable to attack by intruders; such staff could work in pairs;
- teachers are vulnerable when in similar locations; of course, they cannot always work in pairs, but it is essential that someone knows their whereabouts and the time they will finish or move to a different location; someone should be responsible for checking up if these times are not adhered to;
- the provision of nearby, well-lit or controlled car parking;
- well-lit paths across the grounds;
- on larger campuses, the use of security staff, particularly when premises are isolated, few people are actually working, at night, in areas of high risk or where services are prone to attack;
- alarm systems that can be activated in parts of the premises not in use while other parts are in use;
- panic buttons or alarms that can be activated in parts of premises in use even when the main alarm system is unarmed;
- ensuring people work in pairs at least, and that they know who else is/should be on the premises;
- making sure that people are aware of any callers, contractors, deliveries and so on that are expected.

References

1   Elton Committee (1989), *Discipline in Schools – Report of the Committee of Inquiry Chaired by Lord Elton* (The Elton Report), London: HMSO.
2   Department of Education and Science (1987), *Building Bulletin 67: Crime Prevention in Schools*, London: DES.

11 Residential education establishments

When discussing the subject of staff safety at the Headmasters' and Headmistresses' Conference, it became clear that most boarding schools have built up centuries of boarding experience together with the associated problems. With some independent boarding schools, the common attitude appeared to be that schools should be left to their own devices: 'good common sense is applied', and in any event, these schools experienced 'very few problems. Boarding schools, after all, are often in the midst of parklands or within easy reach of small country towns where life is safer, isn't it?' The principal occasions when staff or pupils were acknowledged to be vulnerable were when they were on outside visits.

Though the Children Act (1989) resulted in some useful guidelines being produced (usually specific only to the school which wrote them), it is questionable whether most trustees, governors, managers and heads have fully understood the possible repercussions of underestimating the problem of personal safety.

Boarding schools, together with other older residential educational institutions, share problems peculiar to their age and history. Many colleges, universities, special schools and training venues are housed in huge Victorian piles or within the grandeur of stately homes. Many have valuable art collections, decorated ceilings and vast grounds. However, these pre-war and post-war buildings and their environments often illustrate the problems of failing to design for safety. Little thought was given to the possibilities of aggressive intruders, for instance, or that security problems would result from the many entrances and the fact that the main reception areas might be on split sites. For safety's sake, appropriate efforts need to be made to bring the architecture of the past into line with the demands of the modern world.

Most of these worthy establishments are safe, happy and well-run places. However, it is not good business practice to be complacent, and these days, the business of providing private education is very competitive indeed. It is not often recognized that looking after the personal safety of both staff and 'customers' is a cost-cutting exercise.

Safety care is not a matter of choice

It is vital that trustees, governors and managers fully appreciate the consequences should one of their members of staff suffer from violence or aggression of any kind. Attention from the Health and Safety Executive resulting from a claim from someone who has been hurt can result in bad publicity, and can prove very expensive indeed. To refer back to Chapters 5 and 6, it is now mandatory for every employer to undertake risk assessment, and to address the risks by providing training to all staff, as well as instituting procedures and practices.

Only when an employer has fulfilled these legal obligations for all their staff – which, of course, not only includes the teachers but also the bursar, cook, gardener, part-time helpers, and so on – can the employer expect those employees to play their part in ensuring that they do not risk their own or their colleagues' safety, nor that of the school in which or with which they work. If employees then fail to play their part, it is their own insurance claim which is at risk if they run into a problem.

The employer has a duty of care and concern for the students. The ethos and culture of a safety-conscious environment also has the added benefit of enabling pupils and staff to absorb and practise safe behaviour as a matter of course. This is likely to stand them all in good stead for life.

Risk assessment – proving it is worth it

Many educational establishments where The Suzy Lamplugh Trust has been invited to send a speaker, have started to put in place some worthwhile measures to improve the safety and security of staff and pupils. However, at present, the lack of many examples of good practice in risk assessment or incident figures at residential establishments makes it difficult to assess the likelihood of incidents happening. It might therefore be interesting to look at the results obtained by one NHS trust.[1] In this particular case, the assessor from The Suzy Lamplugh Trust discussed the assessment with the managers and decided to concentrate on the following areas: access, communication systems, reception, safety equipment, safe working practices, travel/out visits, training, reporting of incidents, and care of staff following an incident.

Members of staff were asked to identify possible hazards and estimate the likelihood and severity of an occurrence. These covered such areas as:

- working in isolation;
- conducting interviews;
- informing others of where they are and who they are with;
- the ability to summon help, to be seen;
- the public having easy access;
- visitors being identified;
- any worrying situations;
- crossing the campus in the dark;
- car parking.

The findings were that staff:

- are aware of certain risks, but underestimate other risks;
- take a pragmatic approach to personal safety;
- are lacking in knowledge of communication systems;
- are unclear on the use of personal alarms;
- may not be reporting incidents;
- would welcome training.

However, it was the difference between the staff estimate of problems and the actual incidents which proved most informative. Both managers and staff had thought that vandalism and theft were by far their greatest problems. In reality serious physical assault was on a par with theft, and serious verbal abuse and intimidation almost matched the level of vandalism.

The follow-up was rewarding. Not only did the staff welcome the assessment and the report, they felt cared for, informed and more confident. Working as a team, using suggestions similar to those which can be found in this book, they helped the management create procedures and ensured the policy was up-to-date and adhered to. The added bonus was more than worthwhile. Their insurance company reduced their premium by £50,000 per year!

Guidelines for staff in residential accommodation

Given the understandable public sensitivity to the issue of relationships between staff and pupils, it is important that staff should have the security of agreed guidelines, especially in carrying out boarding duties. In co-educational boarding schools, staff must, of course, exercise close and appropriate control of the boys and girls under their charge. This includes supervision of dormitory areas.

On the other hand, it is vital to remain aware of the virtue of sound relationships, sensible practices and of the possibility of misunderstandings and even malicious allegations. The following guidelines, which are used by the Headmasters' and Headmistresses' Conference as illustrations of the ways in which some schools are tackling the problem, are offered as an aid to finding the required balance in this difficult but important area:

When not on specific duty

Male members of staff are free to enter boys' boarding areas at any time (to leave a message etc.) and should do so if they hear a disturbance or have any other misgivings. However each House has its own House Master and House Tutor and other members of staff should communicate directly with them about any matters of concern.

In the normal course of events male members of staff should not enter girls' houses. If they are concerned about possible disorder they should notify a female member of staff or a girl prefect as soon as possible. Only if there is clear evidence that a boy has entered a girls' house or if there is an obvious crisis should a male member of staff intrude, and then he should if at all possible be accompanied by a female member of staff, prefect or house captain.

For female members of staff the above guidelines also apply in reverse.

When on duty

There are two particular situations which might give rise to concern:

(a)   One to one encounters between staff and single pupils should, if possible, take place on neutral territory (a public room or area in a boarding house) or, where appropriate in the pupil's own private space. Pressure of room-space may occasionally necessitate such encounters in staff study/bedrooms, but when this occurs an open door is advised, if only to prevent misunderstandings.

(b)   The presence of a member of staff of one sex should not intrude into an area where members of the opposite sex are changing for games or other activities, washing, showering and visiting the washrooms and lavatories, or preparing for bed or having gone to bed.

Staff should only visit dormitories of the other sex during prep and then only those dormitory areas which include prep workplaces. These visits should be regular and well publicised.

Girls who are sent to early bed in the dormitories which include prep workplaces must inform the male M.O.D. [Master on Duty] before going to bed so that discretion may be exercised by both parties.

Public areas within House and House Common Rooms may be visited freely by M.O.Ds of either sex.

Washing/showering and lavatory areas in girls' houses should only be visited in direst emergency (e.g. fire – attempted suicide – burst pipes etc.!) by a male M.O.D or House Master and only then with another senior person.

In Girls' Houses, where a husband and wife team may operate in loco parentis, or where the husband of the Housemistress may be in residence, it is impossible to give an undertaking that they will never be in the girls' boarding section of the house or even in the study/dormitory areas. However in order to ensure privacy for the girls, the husband of the husband and wife team should not enter the dormitory areas, this should be the sole concern of the Housemistress.

Tutoring or pastoral counselling of the girls by male teachers, House Tutors and House Masters should take place in a room set aside for such a purpose, or in a common room, which of course must never be locked.

During times of sickness or 'flu when the number of pupils ill requires that a dormitory be taken over for sick people, visits by duty staff to dormitory areas of the opposite sex should be suspended, except when acting as assistants to the medical staff, when due discretion should be exercised.

Matrons have for years had access to all parts of boys' houses, including dormitories. Female duty staff need to show the same discretion but not be inhibited from being present as required by their duties, particularly when checking during prep time.

All staff act sensitively and responsibly in order to protect themselves from misunderstandings and also in case, as sometimes happens, a pupil conceives a dangerous enthusiasm for a member of staff.[2]

Residential sixth form colleges – personal safety is of equal concern

Increasingly, many boy's schools are accepting girls into their sixth form. In many cases, this has undoubtedly improved the social ethos of the schools and added some stimulating competition and preparation for university and life in general after school. However, the new mix can also be divisive, especially in the area of personal safety.

The macho image of the powerful, all-conquering male can be very strong (particularly in formerly military-dominated schools). Boys are often envisaged as strong, silent and able to deal with any threat to their person. Sometimes as a result of overanxious parents, girls are regarded as vulnerable, fragile and in need of extra protection.

This gives a totally unreal picture. As was emphasized earlier in this book, boys are much more likely to be attacked than girls. Yet there are instances where boys are allowed out much later, especially at weekends, to go into town, for example, than girls. Girls may well see this as discrimination, and understandably, can become very annoyed and are occasionally provoked into taking unreasonable and possibly unsafe actions which are purely a sign of rebellion. Boys, lacking the usual caution of girls, egged on by each other, can get into serious problems in town.

It is important to find a solution which means that both boys and girls have to abide by the same regulations. As far as possible, these regulations should also apply to the teachers on duty. A safety ethos is important for everyone, and teachers need to be natural role models to help ensure that all pupils gain an awareness of and attitude to personal safety which can be a lifelong asset.

Town and gown

All schools suffer from rivalry, or even jealousy, between each other. For instance, pupils may hang around as day schools emerge, waiting to jibe at each other. It is a game which can get out of hand.

In boarding schools, this effect can be very marked and uncomfortable, both for pupils and teachers. It is very tempting, and somewhat exciting, to join in the fray. However, these 'matches' can become quite confrontational and dangerous, especially if drugs, alcohol or weapons are involved.

Colleges and universities also face some uncomfortable 'town and gown' problems of aggression and intimidation. In some universities, students no longer wear their gowns off campus. Indeed, throughout the UK, there are reports of university personnel being targeted. Viewed as 'easy meat', with readily available credit cards, money and electronic gadgets, students are mugged and their lodgings burgled.

Student-bashing is more likely when the university buildings dominate a comparatively small city or town. Staff can find themselves caught up in the same unpleasant and fear-inducing climate. Students may be unfairly seen as wealthy, arrogant, feather-bedded and overprivileged.

However, some universities have slowly but surely begun to address this problem. Those universities least troubled by violence claim to have built bridges to the local community that defuse friction. One university has opened a night club for locals and students.

Universities have also found that installing closed-circuit TV has increased confidence. Many now run a late-night minibus service (which too many students still manage to miss); others supply free personal attack alarms. All these moves also help the staff. The provision of open, subsidized personal safety courses is, of course, invaluable.

References

1   Moore, W. (1996), 'A violent occupation', The *Guardian*, 17 April.

12 Out and about

Meetings, excursions and expeditions

Many people in the education sector will be required to travel with children to outside venues, to make home visits or attend meetings in a variety of settings. Their work may also involve overnight stays in hotels.

Meetings

Clearly, most educational establishments ensure that when staff leave the premises to attend meetings, someone in authority knows exactly where they are going, how they intend to get there and approximately when they are due to return. Most schools also have central points where staff can sign in and out. These simple, precautionary arrangements mean that the alarm can be raised if staff are overdue.

Excursions

Taking a group of students on an excursion can often be viewed by the public as a 'soft option' – a free and easy event, with the 'Mary Poppins crocodile' of obedient young people or dynamically interested and involved older students heading purposefully towards an exhibition, a horticultural eco-logical display, a theatre, a lecture, a concert, an excavation of Roman remains or the Natural History Museum.

Teachers know only too well that excursions bring added strain and stress, and that ensuring things go well through careful planning and thorough preparation is extremely hard work. The words *'in loco parentis'* take on heightened significance when teachers and children are away from their normal environment.

It is not the purpose of this chapter to reiterate DfEE guidelines on excursions and expeditions, nor to duplicate the advice of local education authorities or teachers' associations. However, the following advice when teachers and students are involved in activities outside school may be useful.

Look confident

- Present an image of non-vulnerability: personal safety courses should help everyone to walk with a sense of purpose, look where they are going, and keep their mind on their surroundings.
- All young pupils should have undertaken road safety courses.

Take some simple precautions

- If the students are carrying work material, this is safer and more comfortable if it is in a backpack, securely fitted and closed.
- All money should be hidden discreetly: zip armlets or money belts are ideal.
- Make sure that students can be identified readily (e.g. uniform, school badges), and count them regularly to ensure all are still present.
- No student should display their name clearly on their clothing. It is all too easy to isolate one person from a group with a friendly, seemingly personal call.
- Avoid 'spur of the moment' decisions: hasty ideas can lead to unforeseen problems.
- Think things through thoroughly. Pose the questions: 'If this happened ... What would we do ... ? What *should* we do ... ?'

Never assume you will not meet risks

- Nobody is invulnerable. Even though the chances are slight, be ready for emergencies.
- Discuss with the group what actions might be taken if there was a problem.
- Limit any panic by making clear who is in charge of which groups. Consider who might call the relevant authorities, telephone the school/ college, etc.

If travelling by minibus, plan ahead what you would do if it broke down

- In the event of an accident or breakdown, the *Highway Code*, Section 173, advises you to decide whether or not to stay in the minibus or leave it and stand on the verge. However, 10 per cent of all fatal motorway accidents take place when a vehicle collides with a stationary vehicle parked on the hard shoulder. In 1988, 25 such fatal accidents occurred in this way.

- The advice from the Department of Transport, the police, the RAC and the AA is to stay on the verge, only re-entering the vehicle if you feel in danger. However, with a group of young people, you may need to take other factors into consideration: the weather (fog, rain, snow, sunshine), the time of day, whether it is a dark, deserted country stretch or a busy, well-lit urban area and the question of controlling a young group waiting on the verge. This is not an easy decision. If you do not have a hired driver, the person driving should have completed an approved training course.

Expeditions

Outward-bound trips are character- and team-building exercises which enhance fitness, strength, co-ordination and communication. They are strenuous and usually extremely well organized. However, as has been shown by some appalling accidental deaths of young people taking part, the organizations offering these courses need to be checked and monitored very carefully.

There has also been a dramatic increase in international travel by young people in the last decade. Cheaper travel and simple means of transferring money bring more and more exotic destinations within easy reach, and make it possible to stay for longer periods.

Many young people gain their first experience of being abroad without their parents through a school trip. Most of these expeditions have a serious objective. However, the excitement can produce the illusion of being on holiday and being removed from reality.

For the people who are responsible for conducting such a trip, the legal responsibilities are onerous, and some of the fears of threat to personal safety might appear to be more realistic. Few educational establishments do not shudder over the reports of a tragic Alpine incident, two schoolgirls raped in Africa, young teenagers caught with drugs in their bags, and so on.

Statistically, although increasing, the incidence of problems is very small. Fortunately, there are some useful steps which can not only reduce the risks, but also inform and increase interest both in the trip itself and also the place visited. As experienced teachers know, it is important to:

- prepare for the trip – effectively and carefully;
- on the move – respond with sensitivity and awareness;
- when things go wrong – have the capacity to respond calmly, efficiently and authoritatively.

Many schools will already be reinforcing some of the essential elements which students need to learn if they are to accept responsibility for themselves while enjoying the privilege of going abroad, such as personal, social and health education in the context of other countries (e.g. drugs, alcohol and attitudes to gender).

Pastoral care – in particular, to counteract bullying

Schools will usually have an anti-bullying policy. However, the travelling group need to agree their own policy, which will enable them to discuss the stresses and strains of being together at close quarters, away from home, eating unusual food, and often experiencing different climates. They need to decide between them why they disapprove of bullying and other forms of aggression against their peers, and what non-confrontational action they intend to take.

Preparation tasks for group discussion

- **Belongings** – how to avoid looking like a tourist (by avoiding wearing new clothes, including shoes, and carrying the kind of belongings for which they are likely to be mugged);
- **Health** – inoculations, first aid, emergency kits, fitness, dental health check-ups;
- **Money/documentation** – preparations, telephone charge cards, Visa cards;
- **Culture** – find out about the country (from books, embassies, magazines, the Foreign Office), understanding other cultures' body language, rules of behaviour and dress codes;
- **Security** – light luggage, concealed valuables pouches, waistband pouches for day-to-day needs, inexpensive but suitable clothes; military-style clothing and equipment should *never* be used.

For up-to-date safety information, The Suzy Lamplugh Trust, through Oxford Brookes University, has pages on every country in the world. This is being made accessible from the Internet and will provide instant, useful data on personal safety, including emergency numbers, British embassy and tourist office addresses, telephone and fax numbers, as well as safe transport, legal systems, women in society, prohibited items, dress codes, specific dangers, etc. These pages are an invaluable asset both for planning and in an emergency.[1] (Further details are available from The Suzy Lamplugh Trust.)

References

1 Oxford Brookes University School of Planning (1994), *A Guide to Personal Safety for Young Travellers Abroad*, Oxford Brookes University.

13 Interviews and home visits

People who work in education, through the very nature of their work, are bound to be regularly involved in conducting interviews. With most teachers, many of the skills needed for this sensitive task develop over time, with experience and the confidence that comes with dealing with people, especially the more difficult pupils and their families. It goes without saying that the skills needed for successful interviewing are also the skills which will keep us safe in situations in which we are faced with aggressive behaviour.

In today's climate of concern, education establishments might find it profitable to review the advice they give to staff on how to interview successfully, and to consider whether training can be provided which will enhance each individual's communication skills – a most necessary part of the teacher's expertise.

It is fair to say that to date, establishments have usually offered training to inexperienced members of staff through 'on-the-job' training, usually through the observation of a more senior member of staff at work in the interview situation and by ensuring the inexperienced members of staff do not face difficult interviews unsupported.

With the enormous pressures on training budgets caused by the need to set in place the National Curriculum over the last decade, schools in particular might be forgiven for feeling that at present, they are no longer able to do the job of providing help, support and training for the inexperienced in what are, after all, the fundamental skills needed to become successful practitioners. We need to ask ourselves whether renewed emphasis on this type of training is not urgently needed. Several avenues could be explored:

- revise the initial teacher training curriculum of student teachers to incorporate interview training and role-plays in the communication training module of the basic teachers' curriculum;
- through in-service training, address the problems of professionals in

dealing with violence and aggression within their work setting; training courses should be led by suitably qualified professionals, with regular updates.

In the mean time, the following ideas may help make effective use of interviews and reduce opportunities for misunderstanding and frustration, especially when angry parents visit the school.

Guidelines for interviews

Preparation is an essential ingredient in ensuring that interviews prove constructive rather than confrontational. When assessing the risks of violence and aggression, it is important to ask a number of questions:

- Where do interviews take place?

  - Access: who can get in, where and how?
  - Egress: where are the exits, escape routes, routes to well-lit or populated areas?
  - Furniture: does this hinder an attack, or could it trap an interviewer by blocking an exit?
  - Isolation: can others make contact? Is it easy to see and be seen?
  - Contact: is there an emergency call system – flashing lights, alarm system? Who will react?
  - Personal alarm: have interviewers been provided with one, and do they know how to use it in an immediate situation to gain time?
  - Lighting: especially at night – not only in the room, but also in the corridors, car park, etc.
  - Weapons: is there any object in the immediate vicinity which could be used as a weapon by others?

- What is the physical position of the interviewer in relation to the interviewee?

  - All the seats should be of equal height, so that the interviewee does not feel patronized.
  - It should be possible to sit at a 45-degree angle, as this is less threatening: opposite implies confrontation; side-by-side feels like co-operation/conversation.
  - A desk may be useful for safety; however, if it is too wide, it can form a barrier.
  - Aggressive and violent people have a wider than normal buffer zone and may need more personal space. It is wise to ensure there is

enough space in an interview room, while also making it appear intimate and relaxing (this can be achieved through lighting and warm colouring).

- Does the training include interviewing techniques and anger control for appropriate members of staff?
  - Much psychological research into the types of people who are attacked suggests that the messages given out can have an effect on the likelihood, or otherwise, of being the subject of other people's violence. People who convey by their posture, movement, demeanour and behaviour that they are confident are less likely to be attacked.
  - Sensitivity towards parental difficulties is an asset. Many adults are still influenced by their own school and other childhood experiences, as well as their consequent expectations for their own children. Over-anxious or even ambitious parents can feel very vulnerable.
  - When people are upset, annoyed or frustrated, they are not necessarily in control of themselves or as rational as normal. If they become violent, it is quite possible for the person on the receiving end of their behaviour to make matters worse by becoming annoyed or responding inappropriately. While this may be understandable, it is not very helpful.

- Who is being interviewed?
  - The interviewer will need to be aware that, like most people, children will have given their parents a sanitized version of events. Full preparation and collecting all relevant reports from colleagues will help to present a full picture.

- Is the person known to have
  - a history of violence?
  - criminal convictions for violence?
  - a history of psychiatric illness causing violence?
  - a medical condition which may result in loss of self-control?

- Has the person been known to
  - verbally abuse anyone in the past?
  - threaten someone with violence before?
  - attack anyone?

- Is the person likely
  - to be dealing with high levels of stress?
  - to be drunk?
  - to be on drugs?

- Could the interviewer be seen as a threat

  - to their child?
  - to their family?
  - to them personally?
  - to their reputation?
  - to their business or work?
  - to them getting what they want?

- Is there a potentially violent situation? Someone who is potentially, or about to become, violent can give out signs and signals that constitute a recognizable warning:

  - agitation;
  - tapping the table;
  - loud speech/shouting;
  - muscle tension in face, hands, limbs; fidgeting, hand-wringing; clenching fists;
  - drawing breath in sharply;
  - colour of face: pale is dangerous – the body is ready for action; a red face is likely to indicate a bark worse than the bite, but this could change;
  - finger-wagging or jabbing;
  - inability to be still, even pacing about;
  - swearing;
  - staring eyes;
  - sweating;
  - oversensitivity to ideas, suggestions;
  - rapid mood swings.

- Can the interviewer handle a difficult interview? Members of staff need to:

  - know whether they are in a position to offer the interviewee a realistic and reasonable answer to their expectations;
  - know whether they are competent to handle the situation;
  - be confident that they have back-up;
  - be assured that they can summon help;
  - have a plan of how to approach the problem.

Confrontation in front of an audience should be avoided, particularly in front of groups of pupils. The fewer people that are involved in an incident, the easier it is for the aggressor to back down without losing face. Techniques such as calming, reaching and controlling are helpful. These are discussed in Chapter 17.

Home visits

One of the causes of aggressive and violent behaviour is when people feel that there is an intrusion into their private life. Some staff will need to visit pupils and their families in their homes. This may involve travelling to known trouble areas of a town and/or evening visits.

The likelihood of violence against a member of staff on a home visit may depend on why he/she is there. An Educational Welfare Officer (EWO) providing active support and assistance to the parent of a child assessed as having special needs is likely to receive a very different reception from an EWO who is there to discuss the truancy of a pupil.

Unlike a member of staff interviewing within the educational establishment, the EWO or teacher on a home visit is a lone worker, ultimately cared for by senior management, but immediately responsible for themselves.

Whatever the reason for being in someone else's home, the cardinal rule is to remember that it is *their* home, *their* territory which is being entered. Under 'normal' circumstances, people are in control of their homes and what happens there; your presence may change that. People may feel an invasion of space, loss of power, imposition of rules and regulations or, quite literally, being taken over. Some general points to bear in mind when planning home visits are:

- Is it essential to go *alone* to someone's home? You could consider taking a colleague with you, although this may be difficult when resources are scarce and workloads heavy.
- Before you visit someone at home, check whether that person or someone else in the household (such as an older brother) has a record of violence. If there is no record, ask other colleagues who have had dealings with the person concerned.
- Before leaving your workplace, make sure colleagues know where you are going, what your plans are and when you expect to finish a visit and/or return to the workplace. Also, arrange to check in with someone at the workplace. Make sure you take with you notes of telephone numbers and money or a card for the 'phone if you do not have access to a mobile 'phone.
- Consider getting a car 'phone if you travel a lot, as do educational consultants, advisers, inspectors, verifiers, outreach workers and education welfare officers; in some cases, an employer may provide one or contribute towards the cost of it. Car 'phones/mobile 'phones are excellent confidence-boosters, but remember that they are also a high theft risk, so do keep them out of sight. They are an invaluable help in planning and in letting people know where you are and how you are travelling to your destination. However, in an emergency – unlike a 999 call –

a car or mobile 'phone will not indicate your whereabouts, so it is vital to keep alert and to know where you are – this means watching out for signs and taking note of your surroundings.

- Go in daylight wherever possible.
- If you are travelling alone and break down on the motorway and you decide to stay in the vehicle, whether you have 'phoned the police first or not, you should sit in the nearside seat, keeping all doors locked and windows closed. If you decide to stay in the car, remember that it could be involved in an accident.
- When you arrive at the home, think about its location. Is it at the top of a tower block, down a country lane, in a one-way street? Consider where you should park your car so you can leave quickly, or the nearest route to public transport or a busy, well-lit place.
- At the person's home, remember you are the visitor. Say who you are, where you are from and show some identification if you have it. Don't make assumptions, and remember:

  - Check who you are talking to.
  - Make sure you are expected, or at least that it is understood why you are there.
  - Don't march in; wait to be asked, or ask if you can come in.
  - Whenever possible, acknowledge it is the other person's home and territory: let them lead the way, take your coat, invite you to sit down, introduce other people.
  - If you receive an aggressive greeting at the door or the parent appears to be drunk or otherwise out of control, you could decide not to enter the house, or leave immediately without conducting your business.
  - Take only what is essential into a house; leave handbags, briefcases and so on elsewhere if this is possible. Also, avoid taking anything that you would not wish a householder to see or read.
  - In the house take in your surroundings; if at all possible, place yourself within easy reach of an exit.
  - Try to avoid reacting to the house itself, for example if it smells, is very untidy or dirty.
  - At all times, remain alert to changes in moods, movements and expressions.
  - Do not spread your belongings about; if you need to leave quickly, you will not have a chance to collect them.
  - If you feel at risk, leave as quickly as possible. If you are prevented from leaving, you may need to try other strategies in order to try to control the situation.

Any concern about a possible violent reaction from a family member should be discussed with colleagues or superiors, to consider what steps should be taken to achieve the desired meeting without taking undue risks. These may include allocation of the visit to someone already known to, and accepted by, the parent concerned, or an alternative venue.

There are some key words which can be used to remind you of these safety points: the three Vs of visiting – Vet, Verify and Vigilance.

14 The police view of security in schools

It is useful to develop and maintain good links with the local police, not only in schools where violence is likely to occur, but in any school. Indeed, we feel that the police should be encouraged to call in informally, so that these visits are seen as normal by the staff and pupils. The purpose of establishing links is to develop an understanding of one another's working methods, responsibilities and constraints. Staff morale and confidence can be improved if they see that there is a genuine commitment from employers and the authorities to pursue prosecution in certain cases of assault. Crime prevention officers can advise on the security of buildings. Internal guidance on violence prepared for employees could include information on the powers and duties of the police, and guidelines on circumstances when the police should be called.

Police involvement in schools is essential to the broader development and maintenance of good police–community relations as a whole, and to the reduction of crime committed both against and by young people.

Until recently, the police have appeared to be mainly concerned with advising those who work in the education sector on risks to the school and its contents from criminal damage, burglary, theft and arson. But nowadays, their concern has broadened to the lives and safety of pupils and staff, which can be endangered by the actions of criminals. A realistic appreciation of these factors and their potential consequences is a necessary prerequisite for the design of effective safeguards.[1] After all, a successful criminal attack on a school will have at least one of several predictable results:

- loss of equipment;
- loss of data;
- loss of community facilities;
- a drain on resources;
- demoralization of staff and pupils;
- disruption of school life;

- displacement of pupils;
- total loss of the school.

Depending upon its severity, the crime could cause some or all of these effects.

One thing is certain: whatever the precise outcome, any criminal attack upon a school will inevitably impair its efficient functioning, to a greater or lesser extent. Every realistic step should be taken to prevent it. This demands good risk management, as changes in the law and management thinking mean that governing bodies and school staff alike are now more directly accountable for the optimum utilization – and protection – of their resources. The amount of care, attention and vigilance devoted to crime prevention in individual schools is likely to have a major, specific impact on the future availability of funding for their other important needs. In this context, the police view risk management as a means to save money by minimizing, in a cost-effective way, the drain on school resources occasioned by crime. Properly organized risk management leads to:

- improved security;
- a safer school;
- reduced waste;
- increased efficiency;
- a happier school.

This contributes significantly to the school's ultimate aim of providing better education and contributing to the development of mature, responsible citizens.

To this end, a representative risk management group might comprise school governors, members of parent–teacher associations, the headteacher, other teaching and non-teaching staff, the caretaker, and – where appropriate – pupils. The size and composition of the group should reflect the size of the school and the nature and scope of the risk management problem it faces. The role of the risk management group might be:

- to provide a forum to debate and unify a wider range of opinion and experience, and to discuss and decide action on all aspects of risk control;
- to establish a formal organization with responsibility for loss recording, risk assessment, establishing priorities and monitoring the effectiveness of solutions, so that *all* information relating to risk control is co-ordinated and used to optimum effect.
- to learn and develop its own expertise by experience, and to provide a fund of knowledge and an established point of reference for the school as a whole;

- to routinely encourage and assist in the development and implementation of effective loss prevention practices by every department;
- to facilitate safety and security training, raise the general level of risk awareness, and promote the concept of shared responsibility;
- to establish mutually beneficial links with other risk management groups at local, regional and national levels;
- to appoint sub-groups to implement its specific decisions;
- to manage the financial aspects of its operations and projects;
- to provide the leadership and motivation necessary to maintain confidence;
- to identify and consult experts who can give specialist advice – police crime prevention officers, the fire brigade, private security companies, insurance companies, the schools' security officer, and other specialists from the local education authority.

Physical security

This is the first line of defence. Most crime is opportunistic, so a secure image will make many offenders seek an easier target elsewhere. A poorly maintained building encourages further vandalism.

- Perimeter protection is a most important element in ensuring the physical security of the school – 1.8 metre-high metal palisade fencing and gates are most often recommended as a cost-effective and proven means of defence.
- Windows are a popular point of entry for intruders. Ideally, all ground floor windows should be fitted with laminated glass and opening windows operated by multi-point, non-key-operated locking systems. Key-operated window locks should be avoided on safety grounds; so should the use of bars and grilles on secure stores. Skylights should be fitted with internal grilles.
- External doors should be of good quality, solid-core and at least 44 mm thick, if constructed of wood. Glazing in doors should be minimal and of the laminated type. Any beading should be fastened using security screws. Secure them with a five-lever mortise deadlock conforming to at least BS 3621 specification. Fix two mortise bolts, one one-third from the top and the other one-third from the bottom of each door. All outward-opening doors should have hinge bolts fitted to prevent them being lifted out of the frame, and there should be no handles on the outside. Fire exits should not be locked – check security arrangements with the fire brigade. Door frames should be secured to the fabric of the building, using at least 6 inch screws.

- Consider the use of anti-scaling obstacles, for walls and roofs, anti-climbing substances for drainpipes, but remember always to post warning notices and check with the local planning authority.
- Anti-graffiti paint can be applied to walls, so that any graffiti can be easily removed.
- Trees and foliage plants near the building should be trimmed to a low height to allow surveillance and to avoid providing a climbing aid at vulnerable points. Clean and well-kept surroundings are in themselves a deterrent.
- Security lighting can be linked to PIRs (passive infra-red detectors), as they are both energy-efficient and effective.

Internal losses always cause great ill feeling among staff. The following suggestions will improve security:

- Install a safe, and always secure cash and valuables.
- Control the issue of all keys.
- Provide lockers for personal possessions.
- Record serial numbers, property-mark items clearly, and use anchor pads to secure computers, etc.
- Discourage pupils and staff from taking valuable possessions or money to school.
- Keep store cupboards, stationery stores, etc. locked.
- Walk-in thefts are a common offence. Permitting unobserved visitors almost constitutes an open invitation to crime. Ensure all visitors are identified as authentic and given visitor passes.
- Never allow property to be removed for repair or otherwise, without checking the caller's authority.

School Watch

Formal associations between schools and their immediate community have proven effective in reducing local crime by:

- giving early warning of suspicious activity through established 'ring-round', paging or radio link schemes;
- providing a link with local police 'beat officers' and a means of sharing news of crime trends and crime prevention developments;
- establishing a platform to press for improved services in relevant areas such as public lighting;
- assisting you in setting objectives and a strategy for crime prevention.

Calling the police

Make sure all your staff know the local police station telephone number for routine enquiries, but *never be afraid to dial 999.*

Fast, accurate information is the key to dealing with suspicious activity and catching offenders. It is vital to remember to note:

- descriptions of people, their clothes and any distinguishing marks;
- descriptions and registration numbers of any vehicles used, and direction of travel;
- any words spoken, details of accent, etc.

Preventing arson

Arson may follow a chain of events such as a deterioration in the local environment, a build-up of graffiti and other vandalism, and very often a series of break-ins and smaller fires.

- Secure all buildings when not in use.
- Lock waste bins in a secure compound away from the building.
- Chemicals and flammable substances should be locked in a secure store.
- It should be possible to turn off the gas supply in laboratories independently of the supply to the rest of the premises.

Observation

Observation is extremely valuable in establishing who in the vicinity might possibly pose a threat. A close working relationship with the community police officer, with a mutual exchange of views, will often give early warning of dangers which, following agreement between the police and the school or college, can be shared with the whole school or college community. Cars which repeatedly appear at the school or college gates whose occupants have nothing to do with the institution should be noted. Reporting a single registration number may be vital, and can make a substantial contribution to pupil/student safety. Staff and pupils should be alert to suspicious activity, such as unknown people:

- loitering;
- displaying hesitant or nervous activity;

- asking unusual questions about the school;
- wearing inappropriate clothing, such as coats on a hot day.

Establish an in-house system for reporting suspicious incidents and ensure that staff and pupils know the procedure.

Electronic security

This provides extra protection and peace of mind, as well as an added deterrent.

- Intruder alarms should conform to BS 4737 specifications. Police-calling alarm systems must be installed and maintained by a company belonging to a nationally recognized inspectorate body.
- If using an intruder alarm, ensure that external 'bell boxes' are sited prominently for optimum deterrent value and that they are tamper-proof.

Choosing an installer

- Check with the local education authority.
- Always obtain at least three quotations for the installation.
- Try to choose a company on recommendation. Ask other education establishments.

The police allow alarm companies which are subject to inspection by independent regulatory bodies identified in police policy documents to install police-calling alarms.

Closed-circuit television (CCTV)

The output from the cameras should always be recorded and monitored as much as possible. A colour system makes it easier to identify offenders.

CCTV can be a valuable aid to perimeter protection, as well as improving the security of sensitive areas such as entrances, staff and store rooms. Access control systems can be useful in restricting entry to authorized persons, both at the site perimeter and in sensitive areas within it. They can also be used to enhance security and employee safety.

Primary risk assessment checklist

Check out the safety of your own school with this simple primary risk assessment checklist suggested by the police.[2]

Are the trees and foliage in your grounds:

1 growing wide, obstructing public view? △
2 well-trimmed, allowing good visibility? ◯

Gates and fencing should be of the same specification (e.g. 1.8 metre high palisade). Are yours:

1 non-existent, low-grade or in poor condition? △
2 well-maintained, model 1.8 metre high palisade specifications? ❑
3 well-maintained, high-specification (e.g. 1.8 metre high metal
  palisade)? ◯

School grounds should be clean and tidy. Is the security of your outbuildings adequate, considering the nature of their contents?

1 No. △
2 Yes. ◯

Are your external doors:

1 hardwood-panelled? △
2 at least 44 mm thick, and solid? ❑
3 steel-lined, where appropriate? ◯

Do your doors have:

1 latch-type or three-lever mortise locks? △
2 five-lever mortise locks, conforming to BS 3621? ❑
3 seven or more levers, conforming to BS 3621? ◯
4 hinge bolts? ◯

Is the glass in your vulnerable windows and doors:

1 ordinary float glass or wired glass? △
2 protected by laminated film? ❑
3 laminated or armoured? ◯

Do you have powerful external lighting?

1   No.   △
2   Yes.   ○

Is the alarm to your premises:

1   non-existent?   △
2   bells-only?   ❑
3   police-calling?   ○

Are your premises protected by CCTV?

1   No.   ❑
2   Yes.   ○

Do you have an access control system?

1   No.   ❑
2   Yes.   ○

Fire precautions:

1   Have you held a recent fire survey?   Yes. ○   No. △
2   Are your fire extinguishers regularly maintained? Yes. ○   No. △
3   Do you organize regular fire drills?   Yes. ○   No. △

Do you have a secure strong room for attractive items, i.e. computers, microwaves, CD players?

1   No.   △
2   Yes.   ○

Do you have a personal safety risk assessment policy?

1   No.   △
2   Yes.   ○

Have you considered security patrols jointly financed with neighbouring premises?

1   No.   ❑
2   Yes.   ○

Does your school display the National Drugs Helpline telephone number (0800–776600), ChildLine (0800–1111) and Crimestoppers (0800–555111)?

1 No. Δ
2 Yes. $\bigcirc$

Are your staff properly trained in security awareness? Do you have a formal visitors' pass system?

1 No. Δ
2 Yes. $\bigcirc$

Have you considered a School Watch scheme?

1 No. Δ
2 Yes. $\bigcirc$

If you have ticked any Δ boxes, then your premises are *at risk* in the area identified. A tick in a ☐ box indicates an *acceptable* approach to security, while a tick in a $\bigcirc$ box indicates the *preferred* approach. Do you know your local Crime Prevention Officer? Do you know his/her telephone number?

References

1 Carter, R. (1990), *Security in Schools: A management guide*, Newcastle upon Tyne: North East Regional Schools Security Group.
2 West Midlands Police in association with Sensormatic (1995), *Knowing your School*, Birmingham: Sensormatic.

15 After-care – help and support

The most sophisticated policies and procedures for safety cannot guarantee that a violent incident will never occur. Since it is impossible to guarantee safety, the development of 'after-care' services that will be available to anyone who is subjected to violence is valuable. Such services ensure the organization is able to respond in terms of providing support, practical help and access to sources of specialist help if required. Some of the after-care services that could be developed are outlined below.

Action following an incident

Shortly after an incident of violence and after any police formalities, the person who has been attacked should be asked what he/she needs. Wherever possible, managers and colleagues should ensure that these needs are met. For example, the individual concerned may well feel the need to leave the workplace at once, and this will involve the provision of alternative staff cover.

Where there has been a physical assault, the individual concerned should be offered a medical examination as soon as possible, even if it has not been thought necessary to call an ambulance.

Debriefing

Research shows that people who have experienced violence need to talk through their experience as soon as possible after the event if long-term trauma is to be avoided.[1] The incident will probably be initially discussed with senior management, but it is important for all education establishments to ensure that a designated person is available to provide support and to allow the employee who has been assaulted to talk through the experience (again and again, if necessary!). It is vital that these supporters are properly trained, and that everyone in the organization knows who has been trained for this task and how to contact them. They must be contactable quickly, and able to give immediate priority to requests for debriefing at any time.

Important points for the debriefer of a victim to remember are:

- Verbal abuse can be just as upsetting as a physical attack.
- Any criticism of the employee's actions with the benefit of hindsight should be avoided.
- What might have been or should have been done in this incident is less important than what can be learnt for the future to avoid a recurrence.
- A debriefer's role is to listen, support and to encourage the person who has been subjected to violence to talk. Do not expect to 'solve' anything at this stage.
- Debriefers need to know their limits, and when it is more appropriate to ask for specialist help.
- Debriefers are not meant to be expert counsellors or psychologists; they are the immediate, first-line help in a process that may go on for some time.

The knowledge that the educational establishment takes incidents of violence seriously enough to assign and train people as debriefers can encourage employees to report incidents and get the help they need quickly. Debriefing may be a suitable way of providing immediate help for some staff, while others may need specialist help from the outset. The after-care arrangements need to recognize this and not assume that debriefing alone will be adequate in all cases.

Discussion of stressful and painful incidents can help those involved in coming to terms with what has happened, particularly where this is with someone who has had a similar experience. It may be helpful to arrange for the individual who has been subjected to violence to have access to others who have experienced being attacked, and who have adjusted and recovered.

People who have been attacked describe a need to talk through the attack, particularly with colleagues who were involved or who witnessed it. Discussing it helps to 'make sense' of what happened and to accept its reality. It also acknowledges that violence is an issue for the whole team.

Departmental and employer responses play a significant part in helping people to recover and resume their professional role. There is a need for re-assurance that the incident is taken seriously, and that there is concern for the individual worker, as well as for the rest of the team. Letters, cards and flowers are tangible demonstrations of helpful concern and care for the attacked worker.

Counselling

People who have experienced violence may need specialist help or help over a much longer period than can be provided by people within the school or college. In some cases, it could prove helpful for the school or college to assist the victim to obtain access to professional counselling. School managers are advised not to undertake the task of counselling themselves. It can be difficult to discuss feelings of guilt, failure and anxiety about job competence with someone from the same school or college.

Providing professional counselling is sometimes an essential part of helping people to go through the process of acknowledging what has happened to them, adapting to it and being able to move on. Some LEAs/local authorities provide their own counselling services. Counsellors can also be identified in a number of other ways, such as through general practitioners, victim support schemes, local hospitals and the British Association of Counselling. The counsellors should have had specialist training in working with people experiencing post-traumatic stress disorder.

Some education establishments arrange for the employee to make his or her own arrangements for professional counselling, with invoices being sent to the employer for payment. Sometimes, professional associations or trade unions may do this, although they will need full details first.

While it will take time and money to provide access to counselling services, this is a small investment if it avoids future problems for the individual and enables him/her to return to work and to be effective.

Visiting staff who have experienced violence

When staff are off work recovering, it is important to keep in touch with them because they may need help that the establishment can identify and supply. They are likely to want to be in touch with work and to know what has happened as a result of the incident, as well as to be reassured that people care about them and do not blame them in any way for what has happened. In addition, the employee who has suffered an assault will need to be assured that effective steps are being taken to deal with the matter satisfactorily in order to prevent a recurrence.

When considering visiting, it is well worth finding out who the individual would like to see and when they would like to see them. Some people may need a few days to come to terms with what has happened to them or to reflect on the incident before seeing people from the workplace.

Time off work

Employees who are physically injured as a result of violence obviously need time off work to recover, but some people who suffer no physical injury may also need time off work. They may need to come to terms with what happened, recover from shock or regain their confidence. Others may prefer to go straight back to work.

A phased return to work can help, with clear management agreement about hours worked and specific duties. The possibility of a change in timetable, location or hours can also be considered if the employee feels anxious about continuing to work in the location of the attack. It is important to recognize that certain situations, such as court appearances, can trigger renewed feelings of stress, and to respond in a helpful and supportive manner.

Expenses

An employee who has been attacked may incur a number of expenses, for example:

- costs of transport home, to the GP or hospital;
- repair or replacement of damaged clothing;
- costs of dental repairs or treatment;
- repair or replacement of spectacles or a watch broken in the incident;
- prescription charges;
- repair of damage to the employee's car.

Formal agreement about insurance or other policies regarding reimbursement of expenses will avoid the need for *ad hoc* decisions and the possibility of inconsistent or unfair decision-making. The first approach should be made to the senior manager. Occasionally, the costs may be met by an employee's professional association or trade union if it is cheaper to do this than pursue legal redress.

Protected earnings

Any employee who has to take time off work will be likely to be concerned about loss of earnings, either as a direct result of being off work for a long time, or indirectly because, although they may be paid their basic wage or salary, they will miss out on bonuses or overtime payments. This is especially true of non-teaching staff, such as caretakers and cleaners.

Reasonable employers would generally take the view that employees who suffer violence in the line of duty should not suffer financially as well. How employers manage the problem of lost earnings will very much depend on the particular circumstances and systems for payments within each organization. In cases where a straightforward monthly salary or weekly wage is paid, this is guaranteed in accordance with statutory sick pay arrangements. Where bonus payments or overtime are involved, it may be necessary to work out an average over a period before the incident, and guarantee it per month or per week while the employee is off work.

Legal help

The sort of legal help an employee may require will depend on the nature of the violent incident and the consequences of it. In some cases, the police will bring a prosecution, and while this has the advantage of costing the employee nothing directly, he/she may get nothing in the form of compensation as a result. There could be costs attached if the employee is to give evidence, and the organization could help with this and/or make good any loss of property or goods. In addition, information and support from a solicitor could help the employee in the potentially traumatic experience of giving evidence.

When the police do not bring a prosecution, there may still be scope for the individual to bring a civil action. Only after other options have been exhausted, and when there is a good chance of success, will a union bring a private prosecution on behalf of a member. Failing this, the establishment could secure legal advice on behalf of the employee as to whether or not a civil action is likely to be successful in the circumstances. Bringing a civil action can be very costly, and organizations should consider to what extent they can assist in bringing such actions, in what circumstances, and the terms of such an arrangement.

In the UK, where personal injuries have been sustained that are directly attributable to a crime of violence, new arrangements came into force on 1 April 1996 under the Criminal Injuries Compensation Scheme. Such claims are not always complicated. However, if the procedures seem too complex, then organizations could offer help and advice through their solicitors to employees who wish to make an application.

Insurance

Employers should carry insurance to cover the death or injury of an employee as a result of assault in the course of employment. It is essential that organizations carry sufficient insurance cover for themselves and their employees.

Accommodation

It is wise to consider the possibility that an employee may be threatened with violence in or against his or her home if the address is known to an attacker who is awaiting trial and who is not on remand. In such circumstances, establishments should make doubly sure that staff telephone numbers and addresses are always held in confidence and not disclosed to third parties.

Other staff

Where a member of staff has been subjected to violence, their colleagues will have a range of reactions. Some may become very anxious about the danger of violent attacks. It is helpful to involve colleagues in a review of safety procedures soon after the incident, and again in six to eight months' time, when the initial shock reaction may have given way to a more relaxed attitude towards personal safety.

Guidelines for colleagues

If someone has experienced violence, whether or not they have been away from work, other staff can be helped to react appropriately if given some guidelines, for example:

- Our natural curiosity can get the better of us at times. Staff should ask 'How are you?', rather than 'What happened?'
- By all means show concern for your colleague, but be aware that he/she may not be ready or able to discuss their feelings or the incident.
- If your colleague does want to talk, accept this. Also, let them be in control of what they tell you. Ask questions sensitively, and do not probe if they are reticent.
- When he/she wants to stop talking, do not persist.
- Do not criticize any action your colleague describes taking or failing to take during the incident.
- If you are at all concerned about your colleague, suggest they speak to someone with the appropriate training. If you believe they cannot do this but are in need of help, you should speak to a senior manager yourself.

References

1   Bibby, P. (1995), *Personal Safety for Health Care Workers*, Aldershot: Arena.

Part 4

Skills for personal safety

16 Non-verbal communication

Incidents of violence in the workplace are very often considered to be occasions when communication of any 'normal' sort has broken down. However, it is important to remember that the violent person could have started out by trying to communicate. The reason that communication has broken down may not be solely that an individual is prone to violence; it may be a result of all sorts of messages they, and others in the situation, are picking up.

As much as 90 per cent of communication is through non-verbal behaviour, so learning to read the non-verbal signs and signals can be invaluable when trying to assess situations for risk, in predicting violent outbursts and in presenting yourself.

The components of communication are often described as follows:

- verbal – representing 7 per cent of communication;
- non-verbal – vocal tone, which makes up about 38 per cent of communication;
- non-verbal – body language, which makes up 55 per cent of communication.

Very many different elements of verbal and non-verbal behaviour are at play in communication. People give and receive signals, whether consciously or not, and these signals can trigger a spectrum of responses, from positive to negative.

Recognizing signals

Knowledge of the elements of non-verbal communication can help you to develop effective communication skills by enabling you to:

115

- recognize danger signals from others;
- avoid stereotypical or snap judgements of other people that could trigger violence;
- be conscious that other people will receive signals from you and form impressions;
- choose to send certain signals and messages through your non-verbal behaviour.

Impressions and stereotypes

On meeting someone, we form an immediate impression of them. Generally speaking we do not notice individual physical aspects of the person straight away (for example, eyes, hair); we are more likely to register their age, gender and race. It is all too easy to make snap judgements of people on the basis of first impressions and our own stereotypes.

Because of a person's colour, age or disability (we rarely see the ability), it is easy to make judgements about capability, to respond stereotypically to questions or requests or to prejudge that person's behaviour. Others will also respond to us in this way, gaining a first impression or pigeon-holing us as a result of their stereotypes.

Teachers may be especially vulnerable to this, because parents' own school memories can influence their feelings about teachers in general. Early experiences can be enormously powerful, and so can culture change expectations: 'I never got a good education – I'm going to make sure my child has all the best advantages'; 'My teacher terrorized us – I want my child to enjoy learning'; 'My teacher was not strict enough,' and so on.

It is important to acknowledge that we all have first impressions and work from the basis of stereotypes. It is equally important to remember that they may be totally inaccurate or irrelevant. Our 'norm' is not necessarily the other person's 'norm', and it is therefore easy to misinterpret the signs and signals.

Avoiding the possibly unproductive – or even unsafe – consequences of this means putting stereotypes to one side, difficult though it is, and allowing people time to make themselves known to us before we make any decisions about them.

However, this approach needs to be balanced with recognition that 'instinct' should not be ignored. There are occasions when, without it being quite clear why this is the case, instinct tells us to be cautious about a particular person. This has been referred to as the 'hairs on the back of the neck' response. Where there is a strong feeling of unease, this should be respected, and caution exercised.

Dress

Many of our snap judgements about people are as a consequence of dress. We tend to make assessments on the basis of:

- smart or scruffy;
- formal or casual;
- appropriate or inappropriate;
- old-fashioned or trendy.

We also tend to react on the basis of what we like or our past experiences; for example, a uniform can be reassuring or threatening. Our assessment of the person is entirely subjective, and may or may not be accurate or anything like the perception the other person has of him/herself.

What is smart to one person is old-fashioned to another, and what is practical and appropriate to one may be scruffy or too casual to another. How we dress is clearly our own choice, unless our job demands specific clothing or mode of dress and we accept that condition of employment. However, like it or not, we must remember that our clothing will have an impact on other people and their perceptions of us. We all have to make decisions about whether or not to choose clothing with that in mind, and decide if we want to try to create a particular impression. Wearing certain types of clothing can convey a relaxed, open, welcoming appearance, mark the person as 'one of the crowd' or send out signals that the person is businesslike, but there is no guarantee that we will always create the impression we wish.

For example, going into a school with a serious complaint, a parent may be faced with a very smartly dressed woman trained to smile and deal with complaints efficiently. The visitor may see an overdressed individual, grinning as if all were well when plainly, to the complainant, it is not.

Not everyone will be able or willing to take time or make the effort to go beyond first impressions, particularly if they are upset, annoyed or angry to start with. They may also be predisposed to misread signals from others. The appropriateness of clothing is thus important: people can be helped to relate more readily to others if they are not surprised or confused by the signals sent out. It is up to individuals to decide to what extent they will accommodate the expectations of other people and the context in which they are relating to them.

The issue of dressing safely is a contentious one, particularly for women. Certainly women should be free to choose what they wear, but it is essential to bear in mind that the intended messages may not be the ones that are received by other people. Although it curtails individual freedom, a decision to dress differently may be essential to minimize risk.

Eye contact

Appropriate eye contact is a very important element of communication. If you look at someone constantly, you will soon find that they become uncomfortable. People do not generally like to be stared at, peered at or be the subject of a penetrating gaze. Too much eye contact can be interpreted as being threatening or overbearing, and can trigger aggressive responses. Too little eye contact may lead people to believe that you are not listening to them, not paying attention or not taking them seriously, and can also lead to an aggressive reaction.

Appropriate eye contact, for the vast majority of people, means keeping it regular, but not constant. A speaker will look away from a listener, but will establish direct eye contact from time to time to judge whether the listener is attentive, is understanding what is being said, to pick up clues about the listener's reactions and to modify what is being said if necessary.

A listener makes eye contact to demonstrate attentiveness and understanding, but can also convey discomfort or confusion, boredom or other reactions to the speaker. People's eyes can be extremely expressive and show humour, fear, distress, shyness, excitement, and so on. Eye contact enables us to pick up these signals, and in combination with other signals, realize how we are affecting the other person or assess how well we are communicating. This allows us to modify our behaviour and to recognize changes in the other person on which we may choose to, or need to, act.

You can learn to convey certain messages by practising in front of a mirror and using your eyes to express what you want. This can be useful in difficult situations, because you can avoid being 'given away' by your eyes when you have learnt to adopt a calm, steady look and can maintain regular eye contact even under stress.

Facial expressions

Our facial expressions can convey a great deal about the way we are thinking and feeling. Eyes and mouths are probably the most expressive features, and can betray feelings that we are denying with our words.

Facial expressions show everything from terror to total calm, and they can change very quickly as our thoughts and feelings change. Reading people's facial expressions can help in recognizing when they are upset, angry or annoyed, even if their words are not expressing these feelings.

It is often possible to see tension or anger building up on someone's face long before they express it verbally, so you can be forewarned of possible danger and take appropriate action.

Your facial expression may also betray feelings that you would prefer to keep to yourself, or you may wish to learn to recognize and adopt particular facial expressions in certain circumstances. You can learn about your own expressions by sitting in front of a mirror and practising looking tense, relaxed, upset, calm, angry, and so on, so that you come to recognize the feeling of each and can learn to adopt expressions that will help you when communicating with others.

Body posture/movement

Posture and body movements can convey an enormous range of messages about how a person is feeling, their mood, their attitudes and how they are relating to others. Sometimes, the messages are intentional, like a wave of the hand, while sometimes they are not, like nervous fiddling in an interview.

Gestures and movements also have acquired meanings that are understood generally – such as 'thumbs up' – or by particular groups – such as secret signs of a gang of children. Some gestures and movements have meaning in one society or culture and no meaning, or a different meaning, in others. All people who work in education need to be aware of the range of ethnic backgrounds, for example, and cultural and religious issues which will affect communication.

In some cases, posture, gestures or movements may have simply become habits, and are not intended to convey anything, though other people may still read meaning into them. While observing and endeavouring to understand the messages given by posture and body movements is important in communication, it is also necessary to remember how easy it can be to misread or misinterpret the messages. Sometimes, it is as well to check your understanding by asking the other person how they feel or what they are thinking. Some of the ways in which people may convey messages through posture and body movements are as follows:

- **Anxious**
    - clenched hands;
    - pulling at clothing;
    - fiddling with hair, pen, and so on;
    - fidgeting, changing position;
    - frowning;
    - biting lips.

- **Depressed**
    - slumped in a chair;
    - downcast;
    - shoulders hunched;
    - not responding;
    - over-the-top bright and breezy manner.

- **Disapproving**

  - pulling away;
  - folded arms;
  - stiff, upright, looking down;
  - raised eyebrows.

- **Frustrated**

  - sighing;
  - eyes raised skywards;
  - shaking of head;
  - jerky movements of hands, such as tapping.

- **Aggressive**

  - clenched fists or flexing hands;
  - finger-wagging or jabbing;
  - shaking of head;
  - arm-waving;
  - rigid posture, tense muscles.

- **Threatened**

  - closed posture, arms folded, legs crossed;
  - averted gaze, head turned away;
  - backing away.

- **Relaxed**

  - open posture, arms at side;
  - smiling, head up and making eye contact;
  - flowing movements, not jerky or sudden.

Learning to read the messages given by posture and body movements can help you to recognize how other people are feeling and reacting in the course of communication. You can then make decisions about your own behaviour that may increase the effectiveness of communication by relaxing, calming or reassuring the other person. If the messages you receive are danger signals, then you can respond in the most appropriate way to keep yourself safe by defusing the aggression, getting help or getting away.

You can also learn about your own posture and body movements by observing yourself; video is effective for this. It is not without significance that MPs in the 1990s use 'image-makers' to help them to create the impressions they wish to convey. You may decide to avoid certain habits of behaviour that convey messages you do not wish to convey. For example, many of us point or wave fingers in excitement or to add weight to what we are saying. Our listeners may well perceive the gesture as aggressive or overbearing.

You could also learn behaviour that will be helpful in certain circumstances. For example, you can learn how to hold yourself and what to do with
your hands to avoid appearing nervous and fidgeting in difficult situations,
such as interviews or when someone is complaining to you.

Reading the messages in posture and body movement is a skill that can be
learnt and applied, but care must be taken to avoid reading too much into
what you observe, or assuming you are always correct in your reading.
Cultural differences, regional differences, individual habits and your own
approach, preferences and attitudes all complicate the process, so check your
understanding with the other person.

Space

Communication between people can be very significantly affected by the
way in which the space around them, and what they consider to be their
space, is treated by others.

Personal space   Each of us has around us a zone of personal space; for
some people, the zone is very large, and for others it is only small. The zone
can vary too, depending on the individual's mood at any particular time. It
can feel very offensive or aggressive if someone comes too close and invades
this invisible buffer zone. Of course, loved ones and close friends are
welcomed into the personal space, but others may not be. The invasion of
personal space by strangers can feel very threatening, create tension or lead
to upset or anger.

If someone invades your personal space, you are likely to want to back
away and re-establish the space between you; if the person follows, you may
end up feeling pursued or cornered. On the other hand, too much distance
between two people trying to communicate can seem like a gulf, and make
each feel as if the other is unapproachable or inaccessible.

Getting the balance right means being very sensitive to the other person's
signals, so that you can be close enough to avoid feelings of distance without
intruding on their personal space. You will often find that you can get physically closer to someone standing up without causing discomfort than you can
sitting down; people generally seem to require a larger buffer zone when
seated.

Teachers need to be careful not to get too close to students when standing
over them to look at their work. This can trigger feelings of aggression in a
child, or give totally inappropriate messages to teenagers of the opposite
(or occasionally the same) sex. This can, of course, lead to unfortunate
consequences.

Spatial relationship   Just as the distance between yourself and another person is important, so is the relationship, or orientation, in space. Sitting side by side with another person is usually recognized as a co-operative relationship, where you are working together as equals. Sitting opposite someone can seem authoritarian, official, formal, competitive or, especially when a desk is used, as putting up barriers. When in a group, sitting in a circle can signal that everyone has an equal, if different, contribution to make.

Sitting in rows in a formal setting tends to put the power in the hands of a leader and leave it there, and makes getting to know people and forming relationships more difficult. The height at which people sit is significant too: try to ensure you sit at the same height as the person you are talking to. A higher position tends to signal a hierarchy in the relationship, even if this is not intended.

Territory   Another form of space around us is territory. It is a wider area or place that we regard as ours and as where we belong: perhaps a room at home, our office or the area around our desk at work. Our expectation is that, as ours, this territory will be respected and not invaded by others. We are all likely to react adversely if we find someone going through our things, using our things or otherwise invading our territory.

For educational personnel such as education welfare officers, who often have to visit other people's homes, particularly where this involves duties that may be unwelcome, it is not unusual to find that people can become threatening or violent. One reason for this reaction may well be because their territory is invaded and they have little or no power to prevent it. If you are entering other people's territory, it is important to realize that there may be adverse reactions, so take sensible precautions, such as not going alone where there is cause for concern.

Touch

As part of communication, touch has an important role in showing love, support, concern, empathy, encouragement, and so on, as well as the simpler purposes, such as greeting with a handshake, or a congratulatory pat on the back.

The acceptability of different kinds of touch varies between individuals, cultures and other groups, and we learn what is appropriate and what is not through observation, experience and reading the signals we receive from others. Some people will not like to be touched at all; they may be distressed by it or feel threatened, and could react aggressively. Some people feel unable to touch because they are unsure of how it will be received, or it may seem 'unprofessional' in some settings, or 'sloppy'. Others, however, are uninhibited and spontaneous about touching. There are also people who may well want the comfort or reassurance of touch but may be unable to signal that is what they need.

Touch is an area requiring careful consideration of the other person's needs. It can be patronizing, offensive, feel like an invasion of personal space or even recall unpleasant and traumatic memories. On the other hand, touch can be the most effective way of showing genuine care and concern for another person and establishing a bond with them.

One way to discover if touch is needed and welcome is to observe the other person carefully while offering limited support, such as a hand on their arm. They will signal their comfort or discomfort, and you can decide whether to move away or put a comforting arm around their shoulders.

Staff who have a duty of care for children should be aware that in most circumstances, it is unwise to touch pupils. Obviously, this would not apply to very young children, who will often show signs of affection to teachers and auxiliary personnel of whom they are fond, like the child who grasps the hand of a lunchtime supervisor in the playground.

Voice

In communication, what is most important may not be what you say but the way that you say it, or hear it. Tone of voice, pitch, speed, rhythm and accent can all play a part in the communication process over and above the words. To communicate effectively, you should avoid the following:

- making assumptions about people because of their accent;
- making assumptions based on nationality or race; volubility or a staccato mode of speech may merely indicate that the person's first language is not English, not that they are agitated;
- lapsing into an authoritarian or detached response to people, where your voice has little tone or rhythm and you convey disinterest or boredom;
- letting your tension get the better of you and betraying your feelings because your voice becomes higher-pitched and you adopt an excited tone or start to gabble;
- using a supercilious tone, as there is little more likely to trigger a violent reaction than making the other person feel put down, foolish or wrong;
- mumbling or speaking too quickly, because being unable to hear properly or follow what is said is irritating and frustrating to the listener;
- showing your views and feelings in your tone (for example, contempt or sarcasm) but *not* in your words; the listener is still more than likely to pick up your signals and respond in kind.

In dealing with others, don't just listen to the words spoken, but watch for the following:

- raised voice, rapid speech and gabbling, as this may signal rising tension;
- changes in tone and pitch as the conversation progresses that may suggest anger, frustration or impending violent behaviour;
- slow, menacing tones that, despite the words, demonstrate that the speaker is angry and likely to erupt into violent behaviour.

One of the most useful of skills is to be able to control your voice in difficult or threatening situations. Tension caused by fear of real or perceived problems can raise your pitch or even make it difficult to speak coherently. Under overt threat, your voice can disappear altogether. If you gently sigh, expelling all the air, you will release the tension, regain voice control and be in a position to react with confidence. This technique is as useful when facing an unruly class as when interviewing a difficult parent.

Your aim is to be calm, clear, firm and polite, even if the other person is none of these things. You can practise this using a tape recorder to get accustomed to your own voice and to try out and learn calm, clear, firm and polite responses. Another way is to work with other people and role-play situations, so that you can practise responding appropriately.

Listening

Listening is an essential part of communicating effectively. It can be passive, but to be really effective it needs to be – and be seen to be – active. On the one hand, active listening implies letting the speaker know you are listening and following what is said by sounds you make ('mmm, yes') and the gestures or feedback (nodding your head, smiling acknowledgement) you use. This confirms for the speaker that you are attentive. On the other hand, active listening is about the process of picking up non-verbal signals, assessing the messages in and behind words, and putting all the non-verbal information together with the verbal to build up a complete picture of what is being said.

Listening actively to someone can be very important, first of all to them, because:

- It shows they are being given the space to say what they want to say.
- They are being given time and attention by someone.
- It demonstrates that what they say is felt to be worth listening to.
- It avoids feelings of being fobbed off, frustration and anger.

It is also important to you, because:

- It allows you to focus attention on that person and nothing else.

- You can concentrate on both the verbal and non-verbal communication together, and form a more accurate view of the problem or issue and the person's feelings.
- It avoids misunderstanding or partial understanding, and so can save time and avoid problems.
- It makes it possible to respond sensibly and sensitively to the other person.
- It gives you a better chance of predicting behaviour that may put you at risk.

Making time to listen actively to someone can help establish a relationship and co-operation. Someone who has been listened to and feels they have been heard is more likely to accept a less than ideal solution to a problem than someone who feels they have not had a chance to explain, or not been given explanations in return. Nowhere is this more true than in the teacher–pupil or teacher–parent relationship.

17 Coping with violence

No matter how aware and careful you are, how skilful you are at recognizing and avoiding danger or how well you implement calming or controlling techniques, you could still find yourself faced with violent behaviour.

There is a very fine line between someone being upset, angry or giving vent to their feelings and violence directed at another person. The recipient will, to some extent, determine where that line is drawn, depending on the point at which they personally feel at risk, threatened or unsafe. In this chapter, we consider possible responses to violent behaviour not involving physical attack, and then responses to physical violence itself.

Coping with your own anger

There is always a time when your own anger can rush in as a response to the anger of others. It may be that you are tired, have met this problem before (or rather too often) or this particular person before. Your own state of mind may be in danger of hindering your ability to act and behave rationally. In almost all situations except extreme emergencies, your goal must be to postpone any resolution of the internal conflict. You need to 'keep your cool' and use your energy to protect yourself, if necessary.

Do not wait for an occasion to arise first: prepare yourself by developing tactics to calm yourself down. The following exercise, written by Gael Lindenfield in her book, *Managing Anger*, describes one approach. She gives some useful examples of positive statements to start you thinking.[1] The list you use needs to be tailored to you and your needs.

Exercise: Positive self-talk

Using your adult wisdom and knowledge, make a list of statements and affirmations which you can quickly bring to the forefront of your mind when you find yourself faced with another person's anger. Make sure that the list is appropriate for you and your needs. You can use the following examples to start you thinking. Feel free to include any or all of them in your own list!

> Anger is a temporary state – it will pass.
> Anger releases tension but cannot solve differences.
> I do not have to negotiate with an angry person.
> An angry exchange rarely resolves differences.
> The best decisions are not made when anger is aroused.
> I am not responsible for this person's feelings.
> I am responsible for my own feelings and responses.
> I have the right to choose not to express my anger, even when it is justified.
> I am able to put a temporary lid on my own anger.
> I can control my physiological reaction to anger.
> I can reduce the stress in this situation by keeping calm.
> I must not expect 'fair play' while people are angry.
> People say things which they do not mean when they are angry.
> I can expect exaggeration and excess in a display of anger.
> I may be getting anger which belongs elsewhere.
> Analysis is best left until anger has abated.
> My self-esteem can survive without the approval of everyone.
> Anger is not the same as aggression.
> Violence does not have to be a part of an angry exchange.
> I have a right to protect myself from the aggressive anger of others.
> I can ask for help if I think I am in physical danger.
> I must not judge a person until their anger has passed.

Read your list *regularly*, especially before encountering situations where you know you may face anger. You could edit the list down to three or four concise statements which you could then memorise and use in the same way as affirmations.

Violence not involving physical attack

If someone becomes abusive and threatening, consider whether or not you can cope with the situation. You should not feel you have to cope with it alone: you can seek help from other people, or leave altogether. First keep calm, relax, allow yourself time to think and decide the best course of action. Ask yourself if what has occurred so far in the exchange means that someone else, specially briefed by you, would be better placed to handle the situation.

Colleagues may have particular skills or experience that you do not have. The situation may be such that it requires specialist help, such as the police to eject a person; if so, you should get the help quickly before the situation deteriorates.

If you decide you can cope, there are a number of different approaches. One that has been found to work well is the 'control trilogy'. It has three stages: *calming*, *reaching* and *controlling*.

Calming

The purpose of the calming stage is to take the heat out of the situation and enable you to start communicating with the other person positively. The principle is to simply accept what is said, not evaluate it or respond to it at this stage. This may still hold true where a child has been rude or offensive to a teacher, especially in front of other children. Nothing is to be gained by responding in a like manner – indeed, the situation may deteriorate. The child should calmly be asked to report to a senior staff member. If he/she refuses to go, the teacher should seek assistance and deal with the matter later.

Remember that people can hyperventilate under stress. Calm yourself, breathe out first, and then breathe steadily while tensing your muscles and then releasing them – this can be very effective and is worth practising. Practise this when you wake up in the morning, or as you are settling before you go to sleep:

1 Clench your hands tight – and release.
2 Push your shoulders down firmly and feel the pressure on the spine – and tighten your tummy as if to touch your spine – keep breathing – and release.
3 Push your feet downwards, and then relax.
4 Drop your jaw and sigh – you will now be ready for living, or alternatively, will sleep very well.

Now think about yourself, particularly your verbal and non-verbal communication.

- **Voice** – keep your voice steady and calm; maintain an even tone and pitch. Speak gently, slowly, clearly and carefully.
- **Face** – show that you are listening and attentive; use nods to signal you are following. Try to relax your facial muscles and convey openness and empathy with the speaker.
- **Eyes** – make eye contact, but avoid constant eye contact that may be threatening or trigger aggression because it is perceived as staring.
- **Position** – try to avoid eyeball-to-eyeball positions or positions where you are higher up than the other person. Avoid barriers, too, if it is safe to do so.
- **Posture** – avoid aggressive or defensive stances, such as arms folded, hands on hips or waving fingers or arms. Try to look relaxed and open.
- **Space** – give the aggressor plenty of space. When we are upset or angry, the personal space buffer zone we require can be greater than normal, and the proximity of others more threatening.

Now think about the other person; do things and encourage them to do things that will contribute to calming them, such as:

- **Talking** – keep the aggressor talking and explaining the problem, their perception of what has happened, why they feel aggrieved, and so on. Use verbal and non-verbal prompts (saying 'mmm' or 'yes' or nodding) to keep them talking. Use open questions to encourage them to talk, explain or even think out loud. All this uses up energy and helps to get pent-up frustration out of their system.
- **Listen** – make sure you listen; the information you gather may be useful. Make sure they know you are listening to them. Listen also for the feelings, concerns and possible intentions behind their words.
- **Hear them out** – let this calming phase go on as long as necessary, so that the aggressor feels the whole story has been told and heard. Also hear them out from the point of view of not drawing any conclusions, trying to assess or evaluate or solve the problems at this stage. Concentrate on the aggressor and what is being said; this is their space, and they will be doing most of the talking.
- **Watch** – as you go through the calming phase watch for changes in behaviour, for example: lowering of voice to 'normal' tone, relaxing of facial muscles, steadier breathing, change in language used, postural changes or increasing tiredness (being aggressive is tiring). These changes can signal that the aggressor is becoming calmer and more approachable.
- **Resist arguing** – it is very tempting to respond and become engaged in an argument, especially if you are the butt of the aggression or accused in some way. Resist arguing: it is far more likely to result in conflict or confrontation than contribute to defusing the situation.
- **Be yourself** – do not hide behind authority, status or a job title. Try to convey who you are; tell the aggressor your name and ask them their name. By using your name instead of a description of your status, you are presenting yourself as another human being. Later, it may be important to explain what authority or status you have, in order to reassure the person that you are in a position to act on their behalf.

Reaching

When you believe that the aggressor has calmed sufficiently (as judged by the changes you observe), you can begin to reach out and try to build bridges to enable communication. You are likely to be talking more at this stage than the calming stage, as you begin to develop a dialogue.

Continue to behave as before, but develop the interactions with the aggressor; you will be able to do this much more effectively if you have listened well in the calming stage, for example:

- Explain back to them what you believe they have said, what the problem is or what they require.
- Seek their confirmation of the facts or key points they have made.
- Clarify what action, assistance and so on they require. Encourage them into further relaxation by sitting down, if this is possible, and offering them refreshments.
- Try smiling in encouragement and acknowledgement, as it can relax both of you, but do prevent them from thinking you find the situation funny.
- Empathize with their feelings, but avoid any behaviour that could be interpreted as patronizing.
- Ask any questions you need to ask, but make sure they know why you need to know.
- Encourage them to relate to you: if necessary, check that they remember your name, your job and how you can help them, as they may have forgotten in the heat of the moment.
- Try to move physically alongside the other person if you can and you feel it is safe; this can signal an intention to work towards a solution together.
- Try to find out about the other person, particularly previous contacts or experience of your organization or other information that may help you deal with the problem.
- Encourage them to ask questions, clarify things or seek information. In replying, keep it simple and straightforward, and avoid jargon.
- Consider taking notes if this gives a positive impression of taking the other person seriously or being the first steps towards helping them. Do not take notes if it appears to the other person to be officialdom in action. Seek the other person's agreement, and explain why you need to take notes.

Controlling

Once you feel that you have established a reasonably 'normal' mode of communication with the aggressor, you can move into the controlling stage. This does not mean you take over and run the show! It means that you can move forward together in a controlled fashion towards a resolution of the problem.

This stage requires you to maintain the calming and reaching behaviour while moving forward to actually tackling the problem. The aim of this process is win–win: both you and the other person achieving a solution that is satisfactory.

As you work with the other person towards the solution, use the following approaches:

- **Set targets for yourselves** – set out what you need to achieve and when (immediately, later, today, by an agreed time), and make sure both of you agree to and understand what you are aiming for.
- **One at a time** – if the situation or problem is complex, tackle each aspect separately. Agree the list of issues you need to work through with the other person.
- **Simple first** – tackle the simpler problems, issues or aspects of the situation first and quickly. Solving parts of the problem or resolving the simpler issues quickly creates a positive atmosphere by demonstrating progress.
- **Complex later** – move on to tackle the more complex aspects of the situation once you have made some progress and are working more effectively together. Try to divide the more complex aspects so that you can tackle them one by one, or agree the steps you need to take and then go through them.
- **Establish reality** – be clear and honest about what you can and cannot do. Explain what is achievable, when, and what is not, and give the reasons; make sure the other person has realistic expectations.
- **The other view** – acknowledge that the other person has their own views and opinions and will want to put, and have heard, their side of the argument or their analysis of the situation. You need to understand them and help them to hear things from your side and understand you.
- **Avoid jargon** – steer clear of educational jargon that may confuse or provoke the other person. Above all, avoid defending yourself or the organization by using jargon as a shield: you will simply alienate the other person.
- **Offer alternatives** – if the other person's needs cannot be met (or met fully), it may help to offer alternatives. Any alternatives must be realistic and go some way towards meeting the needs. This approach may offer the other person a way out (a win), especially if they have come to realize they were at fault, that their original expectations are unrealistic, or their needs cannot be met as they would wish.
- **Refer to others** – if you cannot solve the problem or meet the needs, there may be others who can. Do not use this approach as an escape route for yourself by passing the problem on. Refer people on only where you believe they can really obtain help, advice or satisfaction. Try to ensure the person to whom you refer is available, agree a meeting if this is appropriate, and pass on information that will be needed. If you can only provide details of whom they can approach, then

provide full details (name, address, telephone number, and so on) rather than vague directions.

- **Do not hurry** – even if you are busy, you really must arrange meetings at a time when you can see these sorts of situations through. If you do not, you may have wasted a great deal of groundwork, or worse still, left yourself or others open to future aggressive behaviour. Do not show you are pushed for time or try to force the situation along more quickly than the other person can go; that may elicit further aggression.

- **Encourage** – if you are making progress together, express your pleasure at it, acknowledge the other person's part in that, and encourage further co-operation. Encourage them also to express their feelings, so that you can tell whether they really feel satisfied with a solution or progress so far, or whether they are just going along with it.

- **Contract** – sometimes, it will not be possible to solve a problem or deal with all the issues there and then, as you may need time to collect information, research something, and so on. Do not leave the other person feeling 'fobbed off'; think about agreeing future action as a sort of contract between you. Set dates to meet, arrange to telephone, or say when you will write. Agree what each of you will do. Show that you have a continuing commitment to helping them. If you do make a commitment – keep it. This can be more complicated, when interviewing an angry parent, if the child has to be called in, especially when various versions of an event have to be verified – rather than involving just two people, the process is then triangular.

- **Review** – at the end of the process, go back and review what you have achieved, what each of you has agreed to do, any further contact you have agreed or further targets you have set. If the target is set for a child, his/her agreement is also needed.

The control trilogy is one way of coping with aggressive people. It is not particularly easy, but given time and practice, can help you think through the process of dealing with an aggressor and develop the appropriate skills to manage the situation and keep safe.

You will not always be able to go through the three stages sequentially and tidily. Very often, you will find that you move back and forth between stages. As you learn to observe and predict the other person's behaviour, you can react by using the techniques or approaches from each stage. For example, you may be working quite well together on a particular problem when, inadvertently, a raw nerve is touched and the other person becomes aggressive again. You may well have to go right back to basics and start calming the situation again before reaching to re-establish communication and, ultimately, co-operation.

If, when faced with aggression, you decide you can cope and start working through this process, remember you can stop at any time if you feel at risk, or you can get help if you need it. Using the control trilogy to deal with an aggressor can be very effective, but it is time-consuming and requires patience. It also requires you to put aside your feelings to some extent, and make your goal that of managing the situation and resolving the problem. You may do a marvellous job and still end up feeling shaky, upset or angry yourself. Think about what you need, go and talk your experience through with someone, make sure you report the incident, or ask for more specialist help if you need to.

Finally, do not assume that this method will always be appropriate or succeed. Some aggressors are beyond control – particularly if they are ill, drunk or under the influence of drugs – and in some situations, it may be essential to be able to summon help to remove someone creating a disruption.

Physical attack

Violence can take the form of physical attack. The relative rarity of such events does not mean you should not think about and prepare for the possibility. Three possible responses are: ·

- **Flight** – escaping from the situation at the first suggestion of physical violence;
- **Compromise** – attempting to defuse or manage the situation or come to some sort of compromise by handing over what is wanted and removing the threat of violence;
- **Fight** – fighting back, and ultimately fighting free to escape.

Flight and compromise are by far the safest options.

Flight

Getting away is very often the best form of defence, but escape from attack can be more difficult than it sounds. The effect of a surprise attack can be shock that immobilizes you for a time, and once you have recovered, the chance to flee is lost. That is why thinking through how to react is worthwhile – you hope you will never need it, but it is worth doing, just as lifesaving and first aid are worth learning although you hope you will never need them either.

Play the game of 'If this ... then what?' Ask some of your colleagues to discuss with you some of the incidents which have happened to them or to others in the education environment. Consider together what actions could have been taken or should have been available. Discuss the consequences and your intentions. Then carry this game into your normal working life.

Look at incidents which might occur and decide what *you* would do. Gradually, you can train yourself to act or react instinctively.

There are some fairly simple things you can do to make it easier to get away should you need to:

- Practise keeping calm through breathing and relaxation exercises, so you can think clearly and move when you want to. Concentrate on breathing out, as this releases the tension. In most cases, the tension inhibits the joints and blood flow; this can result in jerky, leadened movements and can lead a person to trip or even fall if they try to run away – walking fast is *much* safer.
- Wear shoes you can walk fast in. They need to be the sort of shoes that stay on your feet and are not liable to collapse if you have to increase your speed.
- Wear sensible clothing that allows you to move quickly, and that is not easy to grab to hold on to you, or to use to restrain you.
- Keep your eyes open in whatever environment you find yourself. Train yourself to automatically register exits, escape routes, places where there will be other people, alarm points, and so on.
- If you fear an attack, be prepared to thrust a personal alarm close to the attacker's head, but remember that to use it you need to be able to get hold of it quickly. They are very loud and piercing; even though you are unlikely to find people rushing to your aid, an alarm let off in an attacker's ear will be stunning. While the attacker is stunned, you can turn away quickly and *walk away fast*. Do not be tempted to look back to ensure that the attacker is all right. If the alarm sounds on one note, it can also make the aggressor feel extremely sick.
- Scream and shout as soon as you are able. Your voice can be the first thing to go when you are in a state of fear and shock. You need to practise breathing out deeply, letting oxygen into your system and allowing your blood to circulate properly so you can think and act. Breathing out deeply, like a deep sigh, and expelling the air loudly in a bellow has a remarkable effect. When you shout, you should shout something clear and significant, such as an order to 'call the police' rather than 'help', which may be interpreted as larking about.
- Be realistic about so-called 'self-defence' moves – it is almost impossible to kick someone in the groin, and in the attempt you are most likely to unbalance yourself. Similarly, kicking shins puts you off balance. Do not imagine you could use your fingers or some object to inflict injury, let alone use them to disable others. Scratching faces, poking eyes out and so on does not come naturally to most people. If you attempt it, you are also vulnerable to having your hands and arms, or even a weapon, grabbed and used against you.

- Remember that lashing out with a bag, briefcase or umbrella may not be very sensible either, since you could end up off balance or have your would-be weapon taken from you and used against you.
- Don't imagine you can run away with all your possessions. For example, if you are carrying a heavy briefcase, leave it behind.
- Distract your attacker long enough to be able to break free. You need to be sufficiently calm and self-possessed to do this effectively.
- Be prepared to hand over belongings, or let an attacker take them if necessary. Some people carry a purse of money especially to give away in such circumstances. Otherwise, carry only what you must have with you. Keep money, credit cards, cheque cards, valuables and so on in different places, like an internal pocket, if you must carry them at all. It is best to keep some money and your keys on your person if at all possible, as well as a contact card, so you can quickly phone the police and the appropriate number to stop all your credit cards.

Compromise

Defusing the situation may not be a realistic option if the attacker is hell-bent on doing violence to you, is ill, or is under the influence of alcohol or drugs. However, many attackers are only driven to physical violence as a means to obtain what they want. You could try an initial approach to defuse the immediate circumstances, and then get away. The alternatives are:

- **Calm the attacker** – try to buy some time by staying calm, asking questions, talking, and so on, until help arrives or you can see a means of escape.
- **Refuse to be intimidated** – shouting back, becoming angry or showing confidence may deter some attackers altogether, or at least give you time to run or for help to arrive.
- **Give in** – hand over whatever it is the attacker wants; it is often sensible to throw whatever it is clear of you, so the attacker goes for it while you escape. Do not worry about handing over your employer's property: it will be insured, and its loss will be far less costly than injury to you.

If you do make any attempts of this kind, you must be constantly on your guard as the situation develops. Always use whatever time or space you can create to your advantage by getting further away, near an exit, closer to other people, into the open, to an alarm, and so on. Get away just as soon as you can, and get help.

Fighting back – fighting free

Fighting back is only a realistic response when you are trapped and it is the only remaining option. If you have to fight back, the aim should be to get away or to achieve any opening so you can escape. Should you ever be in a situation where you feel you must fight off an attacker, the legal position is complex. You need to remember that:

- You can defend yourself, but may do only what is reasonable in the circumstances. The law permits you to defend yourself, but not to take revenge upon your attacker or to use unreasonable force; such action could be construed as assault, as could lashing out at an attacker leaving the scene, so do not attempt to pursue an intruder or intruders who are already leaving the scene. Report the incident as quickly as possible.
- You may use force to defend your property, again provided that force is reasonable given the circumstances. Aggression used against aggression usually leads to confrontation.
- You may use reasonable force to detain an attacker until help or the police arrive. You would need to be very heavy or extremely strong to do this on your own. It would be best to get away or leave him or her locked in a room.
- You cannot carry an offensive weapon in a public place, even if you only ever intend to use it in your own defence (Prevention of Crime Act 1953, Section 1). There is no such thing as a defensive weapon. You cannot, therefore, carry anything made for or adapted to cause injury, and that includes articles that originally had innocent purposes but have been adapted. Note also that *any* article is an offensive weapon if the bearer intends to use it to cause injury. Special legislation applies to articles with blades or sharp points (Criminal Justice Act 1988, Section 139). It is an offence to carry in a public place an article which has a blade or sharp point, except a folding pocket knife with a blade whose cutting edge measures 3 inches or less. But if such an article, including a folding pocket knife, were made, adapted or intended to cause injury, it would become an offensive weapon.
- The law does not preclude the use of innocent items for self-protection, providing the force used is reasonable. Examples include umbrellas, handbags and walking sticks. But remember that your 'weapon' could be taken from you and used against you. By swinging a bag at your attacker, you may be simultaneously presenting your assailant with both the booty and a weapon with which to subdue you. If you hold on to your bag and have the strap round your body, you are likely to be dragged along. It is better to carry some money elsewhere on your

person, and not to fill your bag or briefcase with so many valuable things that you cannot let it go.

- Even if you have learned self-defence, it will only be of limited use if your attacker is bigger and stronger, or if there is more than one person. Some self-defence courses may help you to keep your cool, keep your balance and break free to run, but do not assume it will allow you to toss attackers over your shoulder! Martial arts are sports. Sports or even fitness classes can help you stay mobile, alert, relaxed and ready for action.

- If it comes to a struggle, try to stay clear of even more dangerous spots than the one you are in; avoid being cornered, steer clear of stairways, roadsides, platform edges at stations, dark areas or objects your attacker could use. It is difficult to remember all this in the heat of the moment, so simply remember to stay in as clear and open an area as possible.

- If, as a last resort, you really do have to fight, then *go for it*! Put every bit of anger and energy into your efforts and fight for your life. Forget about hurting the attacker, just do it and *get away*. Try to make the first blow count: you may not get another chance.

- If you disable your attacker, get away as fast as you can. Do not stop to see what you have done or to do more. Go straight to where you will find other people and call the police immediately.

- In fighting back, you risk the possibility of a charge of assault. As soon as you can, make notes about what happened – when, where, witnesses, and so on.

- No one can make the decision for you if you are attacked. It is impossible to judge which is the best option. You are either at risk of death or severe injury (in which case you have *no* option), or you can try the other two options – getting away or attempting to defuse the situation – first. You will need to keep calm, think clearly, act quickly and decisively, and get away.

Physical defence training to combat violence

When drawing up the Guidelines on Risk Assessment, the CBI, TUC and other members of the HSE Committee on Violence to Staff agreed with The Suzy Lamplugh Trust that self-defence courses need to be viewed with great caution. They need to be well taught. However much training a person is given, there will always be times when that person is not on top form. The techniques need to be practised regularly and, even then, avoidance is always the best option. In any violent physical contact, everyone will be hurt, and if an employee responds with active aggression, he or she may risk a counter-claim of assault.

There are other important disadvantages:

- Self-defence can lead to a false sense of security and overconfidence, especially if people do not keep in practice.
- It can lead to potential victims failing to recognize opportunities to calm situations because they are busy planning their defence.
- It is a poor second best to an outcome where neither party suffers injury.
- Self-defence can be ill-conceived and badly taught, the moves unproven, unreliable, and sometimes downright dangerous.

Physical well-being

Your physical well-being can have a significant impact on your safety, quite apart from its influence on your ability to take evasive action, should this become necessary. Noise, long hours of concentration, paperwork and constant planning can easily lead to stress.

Many education professionals neglect their own physical and emotional health. If you are unfit, overtired or stressed, you are less likely to have sufficient energy and alertness to ensure your own safety. You may become less able to deal with difficult people or situations, or more prone to escalate difficult situations into dangerous ones. Think about aspects of your physical well-being: learn to recognize when you are feeling down, sluggish or overtired, and start looking after yourself. For example:

- **Eat properly** – have a sensible, varied, balanced diet. Eat regularly, and take time to eat meals. Avoid too much fat, sugar, depressants such as alcohol, or stimulants such as cigarettes.
- **Exercise** – take regular, daily exercise such as a brisk walk, a daily swim, or get an exercise machine. Half an hour a day can make a big difference.
- **Sleep well** – make sure you allow yourself the sleep you need. Relax before going to bed, have a bath, read or have a soothing drink, but avoid alcohol or sleeping pills.

References

1 Lindenfield, G. (1993), *Managing Anger*, London: Thorsons, pp. 140–1.

18 Developing assertiveness

When faced with violence, it is frequently very difficult to think about and adopt the most appropriate behaviour in response. Often, this is because of the shock or surprise and the emotional and biochemical reactions you are experiencing.

It is possible to learn different ways of behaving and to practise more 'positive' behaviour to a point where you can use it at will, even in difficult situations. One such more positive behaviour is assertive behaviour.

Many people have found it helpful because it teaches them about themselves and their own 'usual' or 'habitual' behaviour patterns; it teaches them about a range of behaviour that they may experience from others, and on a practical level, it teaches strategies for managing interactions with others.

Assertive behaviour

'Assertive behaviour' describes ways of relating to and interacting with other people that recognize and respect the rights, feelings, needs and opinions of both parties. It is an approach to communicating in which self-respect and respect for other people is demonstrated, and it requires awareness and the taking of responsibility for oneself, as well as enabling other people to do the same. Assertiveness is not about getting what you want all the time.

It is salutary to watch the results on both teachers and students who have completed a course in peer mediation. This non-confrontational approach to bullying which is gradually being introduced to British Schools from the United States relies on assertive behaviours and appropriate body language, as well as complete confidentiality. At present in its infancy in the UK, it is nevertheless interesting to note the increased mutual respect and improved communication achieved by the participants.

The concept of assertiveness is probably best understood by contrasting assertive behaviour with other types of behaviour, such as aggressive behaviour, manipulative behaviour, and behaviour that is variously described as 'passive', 'submissive' or 'non-assertive', here described as 'passive' (see Table 18.1).

Assertive behaviour is characterized by:

- self-respect and self-esteem;
- respect for others;
- recognizing your own and others' rights;
- accepting your own positive and negative qualities and those of others;
- acknowledging your own responsibility for your choices and actions;
- recognizing your own needs, wants and feelings, being able to express them, and allowing others to do the same;
- listening to others;
- being able to ask for your own needs to be met and risk refusal;
- accepting that you do not always get what you want; feeling rejection, but not being destroyed by it;
- open and honest interaction with others;
- knowing your own limits; being able to say 'no' and respect others' limits or boundaries;
- giving feedback or constructive criticism when it is due, accepting it of yourself if valid, or rejecting it if it is not.

To sum up: assertive behaviour involves respecting yourself and your own rights while also respecting others and their rights. It requires taking responsibility for yourself and allowing others to do the same for themselves. Assertive behaviour does not guarantee you will always get what you want. It is not about winning and losing, but rather about win–win situations, where both parties are considered and treated as equal and the outcome is acceptable to both – even if one or other party does not get everything they wanted – because the reasons for it are understood.

Assertive behaviour is reflected in the words that are used, but also by the non-verbal communication that accompanies it, for example:

- direct eye contact, but not peering or staring; showing attentiveness and listening;
- relaxed posture, normally well-balanced, not fidgeting;
- facing people at a slight angle – conversation, not confrontation which is threatening; rather, giving them your attention;
- gestures in keeping with what is being said or felt – not agitated or nervous;
- open posture, without arms tightly folded or legs knotted around each other;
- firm, clear tone of voice, but with appropriate expression of feeling.

Table 18.1   Some characteristics of aggressive, manipulative and passive behaviour

AGGRESSIVE	MANIPULATIVE	PASSIVE
Recognizing own rights only	Avoiding direct approach	Acting as a 'doormat'
Forceful expressions of opinion	Covert expressions of views	Failure to express views
Needs to prove superiority	Skills at deceiving	Decision-making problems
Giving orders rather than making requests	Need to be in control	Blaming others
Blaming others	Not trusting self or others	Resignation
Putting people down	Denial of feelings	Giving in saying 'yes' – meaning 'no'
Not listening to others	Insincerity	Complaining behind the scenes
Competitiveness	Making veiled threats	Not knowing own boundaries
Verbal abuse, insults	Using guilt as a weapon	
Over-reacting	Sabotage behind the scenes	
Egocentricity	Using derogatory language	
Threats	Talking behind people's backs	

Assertive behaviour is the most positive of the four approaches – aggressive, manipulative, passive, assertive. Learning assertive behaviour can be helpful in a number of ways, for example:

- When faced with stressful situations, an assertive approach helps you to deal with stress by boosting self-confidence and self-esteem as you consciously acknowledge your rights and needs in a situation.
- Assertiveness can help develop a balanced self-image, acknowledging your worth as a person, your abilities and qualities, without becoming arrogant, while being able to recognize and accept faults and mistakes that you can then work on without punishing yourself.
- Assertiveness can help in controlling emotions such as anxiety, because you can use learnt behaviour to prevent the emotions getting in the way, but without denying them.
- If you feel frustration or anger, assertive approaches will enable the appropriate expression of feelings, rather than expressing them aggressively or bottling them up so that they become a problem later.
- Being assertive makes it easier for others to be assertive, because it is a straightforward way of behaving.
- Demonstrating assertive behaviour can provide others with a model of effective behaviour that they can use.
- Using assertive behaviour in difficult situations can take courage and be stressful in the short term; however, the more you do it, the easier it becomes.
- Assertive behaviour avoids you having the 'left-over' feelings associated with other sorts of behaviour – for example, guilt if you are aggressive or manipulative, kicking yourself if you are passive and give in.

Learning to be assertive

A first step in learning to be assertive is to be clear about your rights and those of other people. You have the right:

- to state your needs, ask for what you want;
- to set your own priorities;
- to be treated with respect;
- to express your feelings, opinions and beliefs;
- to say 'yes' or 'no' for yourself;
- to be treated as an equal human being;
- to make mistakes;
- to change your mind;

- to say 'I don't understand';
- to not seek approval;
- to decide for yourself;
- to decide whether or not you are responsible for solving others' problems.

It may seem unnecessary to list the rights people have, but few of us consciously think about our rights at any time, let alone when we are in difficult situations, particularly if they involve aggressive behaviour towards us. For example, it is difficult to refuse to take responsibility for someone's problem when they are blaming you for it or when you are the representative of the organization they believe to have caused the problem.

Similarly, it takes quite an effort to confront a patronizing senior who treats you as an inferior person, even though you know you have a right to respect and to be treated as an equal human being.

Rights are not one-sided: just as you have these rights, so does everyone else. As with all rights, these bring with them responsibilities: first, responsibility to ourselves to stand up for our rights and, second, the responsibility to respect the rights of others.

Like all skills, assertiveness needs practice in the appropriate context; from that experience, we can go on learning and developing the skills. It is not easy to learn to be assertive or to assert yourself in difficult situations, but once you know the principles, you just have to keep practising until it becomes second nature.

The following examples describe the assertive approach to the sort of interactions we all commonly experience when working in the education sector.

Making requests

- Before you can make requests assertively, it is necessary to know exactly what you want or need.
- In clarifying what it is you want or need, you may have to stop thinking about what other people believe you ought to have. Their expectations of you, or your perception of their expectations, can get in the way of you knowing what you want or need.
- This may sound selfish, probably because many of us are socialized out of expressing plainly our wants and needs in favour of what we should do or doing the things that must be done.
- It is often easier to say what we don't want than what we do want. In the workplace, one often hears 'Don't bother me with that now', as opposed to 'I want you to hang on to that until this afternoon's meeting and give it to me then.'

- Far from being selfish, clearly expressing your needs and wants helps the listener. It is a straightforward way of communicating that does not leave them guessing.
- If it is easier or more natural to start from the negative, do so. Decide what you don't want, work out the ideal alternative to that and what you will settle for – your fallback position – if the ideal is not on offer.
- Decide who you need to make the request to: this must be someone who can do something about it. Approaching or complaining to someone not involved or without the power to meet your request is a waste of time, but a common feature of working life. One often hears people complaining to peers about their line manager – 'I want him/her to listen to me' or 'I want him/her to tell me how I'm getting on' – rather than saying this to the manager.
- When making a request to someone, be sure you have their attention first. It is no good plucking up the courage if the other person is only half-listening or doing something else at the same time. Arrange a meeting time formally if you need to do that to ensure the other person's time and attention.
- When you make the request, do so clearly, concisely; say what you want or need positively and specifically; speak for yourself rather than generalizing, and demonstrate appropriate strength of feeling through your tone of voice and body language.
- You don't have to go in with 'both feet' or 'all guns blazing'; that is much more likely to be, or appear, aggressive. Try starting off requests by saying, for example:

  - 'Will you please ...?'
  - 'Would you ...?'
  - 'Could you please ...?'
  - 'I'd like you to ...'
  - 'I'd prefer you to ...'

- There is a wide range of possible responses to requests, from agreement to direct refusal; some of them will be more difficult to deal with than others. If you get an unsatisfactory response, you will need to decide if your request is important enough to persist with.
- Sticking to your request is one form of persistence, and you should repeat it, perhaps in slightly different but no less clear ways, until it is heard, understood and taken seriously.
- Reflecting the response you get and sticking to your request is another way of persisting, so:

  - pay attention to the other person's response;
  - respond to relevant questions – ignore irrelevant ones that would divert you;

- summarize very briefly what the other person has said;
- make your request again.

- If you do persist in your request, you must keep your tone of voice and body language relaxed and calm. You don't want the exchange to become aggressive.
- Persistence is fine until it becomes clear that to persist further would mean failing to respect the other person's rights, needs and wants. At this point, you may need to accept you cannot have the ideal and try to achieve your previously identified 'fall-back position' as part of a compromise.

Expressing opinions

One of your rights described earlier is the right to hold an opinion and have it heard. When expressing opinions assertively, try to remember:

- You may need to create the opportunity to express your opinion by:
  - arranging to meet someone to put your opinion forward;
  - interrupting if the other person does not give you a chance to speak;
  - writing to someone.

- In expressing yourself, you should make a clear, concise statement of your opinion. Speak for yourself; say 'I think', 'I believe', 'in my opinion', 'it seems to me', rather than generalizing or dressing up your opinion as fact.
- Other people also have the right to their opinions and to have them heard, so give others the chance to speak without interrupting, as far as possible; listen to them, do not belittle their views, and respect their right to a different opinion from yours.
- If someone tries to interrupt you continuously, you can either ignore it and continue, or say something like 'let me finish' or 'hold on' or 'I have not finished yet.' When you *have* finished, you can then ask them what they were going to say and listen to them.
- There are times when it is best to agree to disagree and leave it at that.
- Finding the common ground is a very positive step towards reaching agreement. Try to identify where you do agree, and work from that positive point.
- Non-verbal communication is just as important as what you say; avoid adopting a posture or tone of voice that could be construed as aggressive, especially when expressing opposing views.

Discussion

Discussion is a feature of many kinds of activities in the workplace. We all know how many meetings we have to attend! Discussion can serve all sorts of purposes, such as generating ideas, making decisions, canvassing opinions, testing out ideas, resolving problems, creating proposals and plans or building relationships. Everyone involved in the discussion should have something to contribute, otherwise they should not be there. Thus it follows that everyone should have an equal opportunity to join in fully.

Discussions are often unbalanced, however: for example, with one or more people doing most of the talking and others doing the listening. This can leave the talkers feeling the listeners are not contributing and are selfishly keeping ideas and opinions safely to themselves while the talkers are sharing and taking the risks. The listeners, on the other hand, may well feel they are being taken for granted, not being noticed, that people are not interested in them or their views, or that others 'love to hear themselves talk'.

An assertive approach to discussion, whatever its purpose, can help you as an individual as well as the process of the discussion, thereby making it more effective from everyone's perspective.

The following are suggestions as to how you could take an assertive approach to discussions:

- While you would normally intervene in the conversation at an appropriate point, you may find that if you cannot get a word in, you need to create space for yourself by interrupting. If someone is in full flow, it may be hard to attract attention away from what they are saying. Try using a phrase that gives the speaker a chance to switch their attention to you and makes it clear you want to contribute, such as:
  - 'I'd like to comment on that ...'
  - 'I want to make a point here ...'
  - 'May I just add ...'
  - 'Before we lose the point ...'

- If you need to interrupt, use body language as well to demonstrate that there is no aggression on your part – you just want to speak. Appropriate body language can also help defuse any defensive aggression from the person interrupted.
- When you are speaking, do not allow people to interrupt you until you have had a reasonable time to have your say. Stick to your point, say 'let me finish.' Demonstrate by body language, too, that you don't want to take over but just want an equal chance to put your point across.
- Acknowledge that there may be times when you go on too long and other people will interrupt you for that reason; you must respect their right to a say as well.

- Give other people the chance to respond to what you have said.
- If people are not acknowledging what you have said or responding to it, try asking open questions such as 'How do you see it?', 'What do you think?' or 'What were you going to say?'
- In some discussions, you may have to persist in breaking into the conversation in order to assert your right to equal opportunity of expression. Most people eventually get the message that you want to take an equal part in the proceedings.
- If people do not get the message that you want to contribute on an equal basis with others, you may have to raise it as a problem. Don't blame people; simply say how you feel and what you want people to do differently.
- Should you find yourself doing most of the talking, you may have to stay deliberately quiet at times and/or invite other people to speak by asking questions or seeking a view from them.
- If you are doing most of the talking, it may be that you need to practise listening skills. One way is to listen to the speaker, picking out the key points of what they are saying so that, at the end, you can summarize what they have said.
- Observe body language, so that you know when to stop talking: people fiddling or doodling, slumped in their chairs or gazing out of the window may well be telling you they have listened enough.
- Behaviour in a group can sometimes be unacceptable to some or all of the members: for example, racist or sexist language, mocking someone, putting someone down, covert or outright aggression towards a group member. An assertive approach to handling such a situation would be:

  - not to accuse or blame;
  - to own the problem and explain – for example, 'I am upset by that sort of language because ...' or 'I feel really put down when you say ...', followed by a clear statement of what you want, an assertive request: 'I'd prefer you not to ...', 'Would you stop ...?'

Saying 'No'

Saying 'yes' when you really mean, or want to say, 'no' can leave you feeling exploited or 'put upon'. You may end up resenting other people and getting angry with yourself because you are expending time and energy on others' priorities rather than your own. Responding to everyone else's requests can give you a short-term feeling of being helpful, co-operative and supportive, but you may find you get little job satisfaction from doing others' tasks and have little time to devote to your own job and developing yourself in it.

Eventually, the standard of your work may be affected because you take on too much, and that, combined with resentment of yourself and others, can result in depression. Being a martyr can ultimately bring out the worst in the nicest people.

Saying 'no' can be difficult and stressful at the start, but it gets easier with practice and offsets the longer-term risks of not doing so.

Negotiation

Assertiveness is sometimes about refusing requests, saying 'no', and thus not co-operating. Assertiveness can also mean total co-operation, if appropriate. Between the two extremes, there is negotiation and compromise. Negotiation and compromise are commonly needed in many workplaces in all kinds of circumstances, from sorting out some interpersonal 'tiff' to major management and union negotiations. Assertive negotiation involves:

- deciding on your ideal preference in the situation and how strongly you feel about achieving it;
- deciding a 'fall-back position' – a second-order preference that you will settle for;
- communicating your ideal preference and the strength of your feeling about it to the other person(s);
- finding out the ideal preference of the other party, and their strength of feeling about it;
- taking into account the preferences and feelings of both sides, deciding if/when it is appropriate to reveal your second preference;
- finding out what the other party is willing to settle for; if you have not done so already, reveal your second preference;
- establishing agreement with the other party, if at all possible;
- sticking to your guns about your second preference if the other party tries to push you beyond that;
- being prepared for give and take in the process, but knowing what your boundaries are and communicating them clearly;
- accepting that not every negotiation will result in the ideal win–win result where everyone feels that they have achieved something, and they agree to and are committed to the outcome.

Feedback

Feedback is a way of giving people information about how they affect us, or obtaining information about how we affect others. Skilful feedback is a helpful, enabling, learning process, whether it is critical or complimentary.

Giving and receiving feedback is a form of assertive communication, but it does not always come easily to us. People are often not good at giving or receiving compliments or constructive criticism, partly through a lack of skills and practice, and partly through fear of hurting or embarrassing themselves or others.

When giving feedback, start with the positive. It can help the receiver to hear first what you like, appreciate, enjoy or what you feel they did well. We can easily slip into emphasizing the negative – the focus being on mistakes rather than strengths – and in the rush to criticize, the positive aspects are overlooked. If the positive is registered first, the negative is more likely to be listened to and acted upon.

Be specific, so that you do not leave the listener guessing, and only give feedback on what can be changed. Giving feedback to someone about something over which they have little or no control or choice is not only unhelpful, it is pointless and can create frustration and resentment.

Timing is important. Feedback is often most useful as early as possible after the event so that behaviour and feelings are remembered. However, it is important to be as sure as possible that the receiver is ready for the feedback at that stage; in some situations, it may be more helpful to reserve feedback until later.

In situations where you offer negative feedback, suggesting what could have been done differently is often more helpful than simply criticizing. Turn the negative feedback into a positive suggestion, such as: 'I know everyone was eager to get on with the business when I brought the new head of department in today, but you did seem unwelcoming; perhaps next time we can stop for a moment to introduce everyone properly.'

At the end of a particular project on which a member of staff has worked hard, thank and congratulate them, and then lead into feedback by asking them to consider what improvements they would aim for the next time. This will allow you to follow with your suggestions.

Don't assume the feedback you give is immediately understood, or that the message received was the message intended. Check out with the other person to ensure understanding.

Feedback which demands change or tries to impose it on the receiver invites resistance, and may lead to aggression. Feedback is not about telling people what they must do, but what is preferable from the giver's point of view.

Try to be objective. Offering facts before opinions and describing observable behaviour helps to avoid total subjectivity. It can also help put observations into context and give the listener information about the behaviour, as well as its effects on you from your perspective.

Giving critical feedback

- Even well-intended, constructive criticism won't make you popular;

you need to decide what is important: being liked, or getting the message across.

- If criticism is due, it may be kinder to make it sooner rather than later, thus offering the receiver the chance to do something about it now – criticism should be given in private, preferably face-to-face, and make sure there is enough time to discuss it. It is important not to refer back to earlier examples of a problem, if they were not dealt with at the time.
- Be clear about what you prefer the listener to do.
- Make sure the listener understands the positive and negative consequences of acting or not acting on the criticism.
- If you are uncomfortable or awkward about criticizing, you can say so – for example, 'It's difficult for me to say this, but I think you should know ...' or 'I'm concerned about upsetting you but I feel I must tell you ... because ...'
- You may need to persist with the feedback if you meet resistance and you really feel it is essential to get the point over.
- End on a positive note – thank the receiver for listening and set the criticism in the context of what they do well.

Giving complimentary feedback

Expressions of appreciation would help the atmosphere of many workplaces. When giving a compliment, make sure that it is genuine and not made for other ends.

Receiving feedback

Feedback can be uncomfortable to hear sometimes, but it is better than not knowing what others think and feel. Listen to the feedback, because it may help you; you will remain entitled to ignore it if you decide it is irrelevant, insignificant or about behaviour you wish to maintain for other reasons.

Make sure you understand what the giver of feedback is saying before you respond. Avoid jumping to conclusions, becoming defensive or going on the attack, as all these will deter people from giving you feedback. Check that you have understood by asking questions or by paraphrasing what you believe was said.

If you rely on only one source of information, you may get a very individual or biased view. Ask other people for feedback, as you may find they experience you differently. The more information you have, the more likely you are to develop a balanced view of yourself and keep feedback in perspective.

Receiving complimentary feedback Accepting compliments can be difficult but, like gifts, if they are not accepted, the giver may feel hurt, rejected or humiliated and is unlikely to try to give again. Compliments should be accepted without embarrassment. It sometimes takes practice to simply say 'thank you', or 'it is kind of you to say so', 'it's nice to be appreciated'. You can always say 'I'm a little embarrassed, but thank you'; that way, people know why you are reacting as you are, but that you do not want them to avoid complimenting you.

If you believe the giver of the compliment has an ulterior motive, accept the compliment and deal with the hidden agenda at a separate time.

Receiving critical feedback Constructive, well-timed and supportive criticism can still be very uncomfortable to receive, especially if you have been on the receiving end of damaging criticism in the past. On the other hand, it can be very beneficial.

There is nothing worse than discovering too late that you could have done something better or differently (the 'I wish I'd known' syndrome). Accept valid criticism without being defensive, justifying yourself, excusing or passing the buck.

If you do not accept the criticism, you can reject it without rejecting the other person: say 'I disagree', but not 'You are wrong.' The latter is a confrontational response, inviting the other person to prove the opposite.

If the giver of criticism makes generalizations, such as: 'You always do ...', you can find out exactly what they are getting at by explaining you are unclear and asking questions, for example: 'What exactly did I do or say ... ?', 'Can you give me an example of ... ?', 'Can you describe what it is that ... ?' In this way, you can pinpoint your behaviour that gave rise to the criticism and help identify the emotional effects of your actions on others. If you explain that you need more information and ask questions in a way that is not defensive, challenging or aggressive, you can obtain the necessary information to decide whether or not you agree with the criticism.

Another aspect of questions is that they can help demonstrate when criticism is unfair or vindictive, because the giver is unlikely to be able to provide the information, examples, descriptions and so on to support the criticism. In this situation, you can clearly state that you disagree; this may forestall future unfair or vindictive criticism.

When the criticism is intended to be, or proves to be, helpful to you, always thank the giver; it may have been difficult for them to give, and constructive criticism is a practice that should be encouraged.

Part 5

Training for safety

19 Guidelines for trainers

This part provides general guidance for trainers, and a number of sample training programmes, or 'tasks'. These can be used as they stand, or be modified to meet the training needs of particular organizations and groups in education. In using them, the trainer will need to refer to the earlier chapters. Examples of handouts that could be used in the tasks can be found in Appendix A. The trainer can negotiate the times if the course has to be fitted within the school day: for instance, 9–12 a.m., 1–3.30 p.m.

The effectiveness of a personal safety policy will depend on a number of related issues. The organization, and individual employees, will need to be committed to the policy and to the procedures which have been agreed to make the policy work. They will also need training for their role in improving safety levels for themselves and for their colleagues. Training in personal safety skills is an essential ingredient in the development of a successful personal safety policy.

When establishments embark on training programmes, it is not un-common to discover that the roles of different people in ensuring that the training is effective have been assumed, rather than defined. At worst, there can be great confusion about who is responsible for what, so that learners, full of enthusiasm and expectations, find themselves unable to apply their learning because the support, organizational changes, finance and so forth are not in place. Investing some time in ensuring there is clarity about, and agreement on, the roles of different people in the organization will certainly bear dividends.

If, for example, policy-makers and managers are unprepared or unable to accept their role in financing the changes necessary to ensure safe working, there is little point in raising expectations through training. Similarly super-visors must be willing to support the development and maintenance of safer working practices if training is to prove effective. Clarity about the roles of various people in ensuring safe working is an essential precursor to gaining their commitment, which is itself essential if the training is to achieve its aim.

It is important to be clear about what is, and what is not, the trainer's role and responsibility, and what can reasonably be expected of him/her. It may be helpful to consider the following areas in determining the role of the trainer, in negotiating that role with others, or in communicating that role to others.

The trainer can reasonably be expected to take responsibility for planning, designing, implementing and evaluating the training. However, he or she cannot be responsible for policy development or financial decisions, or for solving the organization's or other people's problems.

From the outset, the trainer should ensure that managers and policy-makers support the training and are prepared to provide the necessary resources and organizational support to ensure that training is part of an integrated approach to personal safety. A senior manager should work with the trainer to negotiate with personnel, for example, on the implementation of outcomes from training. Training outcomes will also help to inform developing policy and practice, and again a route into the policy-making machinery will be needed. While safety issues should be addressed at all levels within the organization, it is essential for senior managers to have a special responsibility for seeing that safety is considered and reviewed on a regular basis.

Values and beliefs

Whether we recognize it consciously or not, all of us operate from a basis of our values and beliefs, and this influences our role as trainers. Our own values and beliefs, as well as those underlying the materials and resources we use, will have an impact on the training and the learners.

Some educational organizations have their own trainers, but schools in particular may need to buy in personal safety training from independent trainers. When doing so, they will need to be assured of the competence of the trainer, and also of the values and beliefs within which they work. If the organization seeking training is within the voluntary sector, for example, the trainer will need to be aware of the value system of that particular agency, and of its special interests and role.

The values and beliefs identified below in respect of safety at work and training people are those which underlie this book. They influence its content, style and expectations of how it should be used by all who work in the individual educational organizations. It would be foolish to assume that these values and beliefs are shared by all.

- Working towards safety is 'our' problem, in the sense that everyone has a responsibility. It should never be a 'them' and 'us' situation, where management are in confrontation with the workforce or unions. To achieve a safe working environment, everyone must play their part.
- People have a right to be safe at work, and managers have a duty in law to ensure they are, as far as possible, safe. Equally, managers have a right to expect support and co-operation, and the workforce has a responsibility to fulfil these expectations.
- Trainers train and learners learn. No matter how good the trainer, he/she cannot learn for people, but can only facilitate their learning. Thus participants have a responsibility to play their part in the learning process.
- Training is most effective when it is learner-centred – when the learner's needs, level of experience, preferred style of learning, existing knowledge and working context are all taken into account in designing and providing the training.
- Trainers are enablers of learning – they are a resource, people with expertise and experience (not necessarily expert on content) in designing and providing learning opportunities.
- Training should be comfortable for people, especially those who come to training events fearful of being challenged, questioned or showing themselves up. Even otherwise confident people can find the new or unusual setting of a training event disconcerting or even threatening. This is particularly important where the content of the training may evoke emotional responses. Trainers have a role in ensuring the training environment is comfortable by being clear about its purpose, groundrules and norms of behaviour. It also means trainers may need to support individual learners in difficulty, or deal with any inappropriate responses.
- Equality is a fundamental consideration throughout training; it should be taken into account in all aspects of the process, for example:

  - it should be offered to *all* employees who work within the organization; in schools and colleges, for instance, the ideal way to implement a safety programme would be to train teaching and non-teaching staff together, whenever possible;
  - a range of food to meet all dietary requirements;
  - accessibility for people with disabilities;
  - services such as brailling or induction loops;
  - resources that are free of racist or sexist language;
  - resources that present positive rather than stereotypical images;
  - timing of training to take account of the care responsibilities of the group;

- provision of a crèche or child care;
- dates that do not clash with religious or other festivals;
- language used should not promote stereotypes, for example, assuming the head or senior manager is a 'he';
- not making assumptions about people, but checking how they wish to be referred to – for example, 'women' or 'ladies'; 'black people' or 'Afro-Caribbeans';
- staff in a training venue should know what behaviour is expected of them;
- the venue should be safe – it should have safe, well-lit car parks, be secure at night if people are staying late, and transport to and from it should be provided if necessary;
- everyone should have the opportunity to express views and opinions and these should be respected.

● Recognizing and using the experience of the learners is important, because it:

- involves them actively in the learning;
- recognizes the value of their experience and builds on it;
- can increase the perceived relevance of training to individuals;
- enables learning from each other in the group, thus helping group development;
- is generally what people learn most from.

● Training should be constructive, not destructive. The training should not become an opportunity to criticize, or a griping session; this may well be cathartic for the group, but it is unlikely to help in gaining their commitment to change or recognition of their responsibilities within the process.
● In the context of this training about violence, it is important to stress that it is not personal, but work-related. The training, while being sensitive to people's experience and feelings, is not a counselling activity, but is about the work setting and the development of safe working practices.

Planning training

Planning a training event, like planning anything, usually involves making judgements and decisions while taking into account all sorts of complex and interlinked factors. This process can be simplified by posing some basic questions at the outset, to guide the planner through planning and to avoid missing aspects out. The following checklists, although not exhaustive, pose some key questions in planning.

- **What**

  - needs have been identified?
  - is the training intended to achieve: its aims and objectives?
  - is the event: a two-hour session, a day's course?
  - can realistically be achieved in this time?
  - approach is best and is possible in this time?
  - resources are required (people, funds, equipment, materials)?
  - is the trainer good at, confident doing?
  - help is needed (administrative, specialist input)?

- **Who**

  - is the training for (adults, particular group of staff, cross-section of staff)?
  - is responsible for what (for example, bookings, printing materials, briefing people, presenting, evaluation)?
  - needs to be communicated with (for example, co-trainers or contributors to do the planning, participants about arrangements, managers about outcomes of training)?
  - should be involved in decisions about the training (managers, participants, trainers)?
  - are the trainers? Why have they been chosen? What is their particular expertise and experience?
  - is responsible for follow-up action?

- **When**

  - will the training take place? If it is part of a series, does it need to fit in with other things? Will the timing exclude people – for example, part-time staff? Does the timing allow for planning, preparation, briefing, and so on? Can others involved meet the timescale?
  - do people need to have information about the training and their part in it? Has their commitment been obtained, the date fixed, and have necessary bookings been made?

- **Where**

  - will the event take place? Is there a choice about where it is held? Will it be in the workplace, or outside? Which is preferable, and why? (Bear in mind interruptions and whether people are contactable.) Does the venue meet equal opportunities criteria in terms of access and services? Is the environment appropriate –

space, heating, light, comfortable seats, noise, training equipment and facilities?
- are people travelling from? Is there public transport that can be safely used? Are there parking facilities that are safe?

- **How**

  - will the effectiveness of the training be evaluated, and how will these data inform future training and practice?
  - will the training be followed up – for example, by further training, supporting learners, organizational changes?
  - will the trainer manage difficult people in a group, potentially contentious issues, conflict, a situation where someone gets upset or needs particular help, the group saying 'This is not what we want', demands for management to change practices?

- **Why**

  - is the training being planned? The trainer should ensure that there is support for it in the organization, and that there are not unreasonable expectations that the training itself will solve all the problems or automatically bring about change.

Once these issues have been addressed, a training programme can be produced. It is likely to include some or all of the following:

- **Aim** – a general statement of the purpose of the training;
- **Objectives** – specific statements describing what the participants will learn and be able to do as a result;
- **Target group** – who the training is for, why they need it, how they will benefit, and how it links to their work or other training;
- **Timing** – when it will take place: dates and times; all the times of a series of events should be shown;
- **Location** – where the training will take place: facilities and limitations of the venue, for example, access; how to get there; where the rooms to be used are;
- **The trainer(s)** – who will do the training: internal trainers, or outside specialists; their names and perhaps some information about them, such as background and experience, should be given;
- **Content** – information about the content of the training;
- **Approach** – a description of the approach to be taken in the training event; this could include a statement such as: 'The approach will be varied, involving input by trainers and participative activities.'
- **Evaluation** – how the effectiveness of the training will be assessed, and when, for example:

- by a questionnaire at the end of the event;
- by peer or self-assessment during training;
- by assessment back in the workplace.

- **Contacts** – the training co-ordinator's name, how to contact them, and also how to contact the venue.

Evaluating training

Evaluation processes are generally used to obtain information about the results of training. This information is then used to assess the value and effectiveness of the training with a view to improving it, if necessary. This is an important part of the training process, because evaluation helps to demonstrate whether the aims and objectives of the training have been achieved. Effectiveness can be shown where training has resulted in changed behaviour or practice, or changes in the quality of service. Ways in which training can be developed or made more effective can emerge, as can problems, difficulties or further training needs.

The appropriateness of training for particular groups of staff or for people undertaking particular roles or tasks can be assessed. Evaluation can also highlight the absence of, or uneconomical use of, resources such as money, time, space, materials or personnel allocated to all areas of safety and security throughout the educational establishment. It provides useful feedback to those who were involved at any stage: for example, by backing the decision to embark on the training, and to those who provided the training, as well as to the participants themselves.

Evaluating training is much easier where clear aims and objectives have been set in the first place. There are many ways of obtaining information for evaluation purposes:

- A questionnaire can be used at the end of a session, event or programme to obtain immediate reactions.
- A questionnaire can be used some weeks or months after the training, to help assess if learning has been remembered and/or used in the workplace and has been found to be effective.
- An exercise can be designed for during or after the training to collect information. For example, participants can be invited to write comments under appropriate headings on pieces of flipchart paper pinned around the room – this is called the 'graffiti exercise'.
- Learners can be asked to comment verbally at the end of the training on its value, and their responses recorded.
- Learners can be visited at the workplace some time after the training and interviewed to obtain comments.

- Discussion with the participants' line managers after the event can gather their views on whether learners have developed coping skills, grown in confidence, and so on.
- Participants can be asked to record their views at a later stage, and their comments compared with their views immediately after the event.
- The group can be brought together again for an evaluation session, and asked to comment on the particular aspects about which information is needed.
- Participants can be asked to keep a diary for an agreed time after the training, to record when/if and how they used the learning.

These are just a few ideas for collecting evaluation data. There are many other methods – some very complex – that can be used, but the most important thing to remember is that there is no point in evaluating unless those responsible for training provision are prepared to take note of the findings and make any necessary changes, even if this means admitting mistakes, poor decisions or performance and errors of judgement.

Task 1 Introduction to violence at work

Aim

To increase awareness of the problem of violence at work and how to keep safe.

Objectives

At the end of the programme, the participants will be able to:

- say what is meant by violence at work;
- identify risks they may face at work;
- describe actions they will take to ensure safety at work.

Time

Two-and-a-half hours.

Target groups

All staff who need an introduction to the subject of violence at work and keeping safe. This programme could also be included in a general health and safety programme.

Resources

Flipchart and stand, pens, any prepared materials or handouts.

Environment

A room large enough for the whole group to sit comfortably in a circle and for people to split up to work in pairs for a short time.

Timetable

1	Introduction	15 mins
2	What do we mean by violence at work?	30 mins
3	Minimizing risk	1 hour
4	Safer practice – personal action plan	30 mins
5	Summary/evaluation	15 mins

Contents

1   Introduction

- Introduce yourself and the training programme, saying what the aims and objectives are.
- Ask the group members to introduce themselves.
- Give any 'housekeeping' information, such as time you will finish, location of facilities, fire exits, etc.

2   What do we mean by violence at work?

- Gather the group's ideas of what violence at work is.
- Discuss what they would include in the term 'violence at work' and what they would exclude, and why.
- Explain to, or show, the group how other people define violence at work (see Handout 1).
- Ensure the group understands that 'violence' is used as an all-embracing term to cover a range of behaviour and its effects (see Handout 2).

3   Minimizing risk

- Identify areas of work you know the group is involved in or familiar with – for example, reception, travelling, dealing with the public,

Arena
Marketing Services Manager
Gower House
Croft Road
Aldershot
Hampshire
GU11 3BR

arena

Arena is the newest imprint in the Ashgate Publishing Group.
It gathers together titles on social work and policy, education and health and
aims to help professionals put theory into practice.

Please fill in the section below and return this Freepost reply card to us so that we can send you details
of forthcoming publications in the areas that interest you.

Name _____

Job title and Institution (if relevant) _____

Address _____

_____ Postcode _____

Please send me information on the books you publish in the following subject areas:

☐ Health   ☐ Popular Culture/Youth Studies   ☐ Education   ☐ Advisory Services
☐ Social Reference ☐ Professional Social Work   ☐ Police/Criminology Studies

If you know anyone else who would appreciate this service please give their details here:

_____

_____

☐ *Please tick this box if you do not wish to receive information from other organizations*

2G007

Merlin Communications (UK) Ltd

37A Market Place

CIRENCESTER

GL7 2BR

'Personal Safety for Schools'

A video-based distance learning pack for Schools, designed to Interpret and Communicate the key messages in this book.

Please send me details;

Name...

Position...

Address...

handling money, supervising children and young people. Go through each area, asking the group to identify risks or potential risks, adding to their ideas if necessary. Record their ideas on the flipchart.

- Go back through each of the areas and the risks identified in it, asking the group to suggest actions that could be taken to reduce the risk or to avoid it altogether. Add to the group's suggestions, if necessary.
- Decide with the group which of the actions they have identified can be taken by them individually or as a group, and which need management agreement and support, or the support of others. Record this.

4   Safer practice – personal action plan

- Individuals prepare a personal action plan, listing actions they can take independently to minimize the risks they face, and any actions they can take to bring risks that need action from others to the attention of appropriate people.
- As the group complete action plans ask them to look through them again and put deadlines on their actions, where possible; this will encourage them to stick to their decisions.

5   Summary/evaluation

- Summary – go back over the key learning points:
  - what we mean by violence at work;
  - areas of risk identified;
  - ideas for minimizing risks;
  - actions people have decided to take.

- Evaluation – either:
  - conduct a brief evaluation on the content and conduct of the programme, venue and so on, or
  - explain how the programme will be evaluated later.

Task 2 The role of employers and senior managers

Aim

To ensure employers and senior managers are aware of their duties and roles in ensuring the safety of employees at work (see Chapter 5, pp. 29–36).

Objectives

At the end of the programme, participants will be able to:

- explain their duties as employers in respect of employee safety;
- identify why action in the workplace on safety is necessary;
- prepare an action plan for themselves to assist in developing safety measures.

Time

Three-and-a-half hours.

Target groups

Employers and senior managers, specifically those whose roles involve them in policy development and implementation who have had no formal training in managing violence at work.

Resources

Overhead projector and/or flipchart and pens, any pre-prepared materials or handouts.

Environment

A room large enough to allow the group to work in sub-groups. An area for break time.

Timetable

1	Introduction	15 mins
2	Defining violence at work	15 mins
3	Employer duties and the need for action	1 hour
BREAK		15 mins
4	Taking steps to safety	1 hour
5	Action planning	30 mins
6	Summary/evaluation	15 mins

Contents

1   Introduction

- Introduce yourself and the training programme, using the aims and objectives.
- Ask group members to introduce themselves.
- Give any housekeeping information, such as break time, finishing time, location of facilities, etc.

2   Defining violence at work – a brief input session

- Explain that the term 'violence' is used in a broad sense, encompassing a wide range of behaviour and the effects of it.
- Using prepared overhead projector slides or a flipchart, show them definitions used by others (see Handout 1) or develop your own to show them (see Chapter 4).
- Identify for the group why having a definition of violence at work is useful and important.

3   Employer duties and the need for action

- Ask the group what they believe to be the legal duties of an employer to ensure safety.
- Using prepared handouts, overhead projector slides or a flipchart, show the group a list of their duties under Health and Safety at Work Act and Common Law, and the risks of civil actions against them (see Chapter 5 and Handout 3). Compare with their list – how accurate are they?
- Ask the group what they believe the consequences of not taking action to ensure employee safety are:
  - in legal terms;
  - in terms of the effects on the organization (see Handout 4).

Record responses on the flipchart or overhead projector – offer ideas or add things they miss.

BREAK – 15 mins

4   Taking steps to safety

- Explain the process of risk assessment, the law, and follow-up procedures (see Chapter 6, pp. 37–42).
- Go through each step with the group, explaining what it involves and why it is important. Ask for the group's views on how (or whether) they could take each of the steps. Do they feel it is a useful approach? Can they add suggestions or ideas for their own organization(s)?

5   Action planning

- The action plans should describe actions that will be taken, by whom, or who will be responsible for seeing they are taken, and the time-scales.
- The actions could range from a management meeting to discuss combating violence at work to hiring a consultant to investigate risks and make proposals.
- The action plans should be achievable, and people should be encouraged to follow up with each other to check on progress.

6   Summary/evaluation

- Summary – go back over the key learning points from the programme:
  - a broad definition of violence at work;
  - the need for employers to act to combat violence at work because of

their legal obligations and the effects of violence at work on the organization and individuals;
– action planning;
– turning theory into an action plan on violence at work;
– action decided upon by participants.

● Evaluation – conduct a brief evaluation using a form or group activity, focusing on key areas, such as:

– most significant learning points;
– what else they would like to know or do;
– effectiveness of materials, trainer, etc.

● Explain what further evaluation will be undertaken, and how.

Task 3 Coping with violence

Aim

To equip staff with basic skills in coping with violent behaviour towards them.

Objectives

At the end of the programme, learners will be able to:

- identify a range of violent behaviour;
- describe potential triggers to violent behaviour;
- describe the signs of impending violent behaviour;
- identify a range of actions they could take in the event of being faced with a violent person;
- explain the 'control trilogy' as a process for coping with non-physical violent behaviour (see Chapter 17).

Time

One day initially, with follow-up practice sessions.

Target groups

'Front-line' staff who deal regularly with the public, parents and children.

Resources

Overhead projector and/or flipchart and pens, prepared handouts and other materials, such as briefings for role-player and observers.

Environment

A room large enough to allow the group to work in sub-groups, or provide additional rooms for this.

Timetable

1	Introduction	30 mins
2	What is violent behaviour?	1 hour
BREAK		15 mins
3	Causes and signs of danger	45 mins
4	What to do when faced with violence	1 hour
BREAK FOR LUNCH		1 hour
5	The control trilogy	2¼ hours
6	Action plans	30 mins
7	Summary/evaluation	30 mins

Contents

1   Introduction

- Introduce yourself and the training programme, using the aim and objectives to explain the content and outcomes.
- Ask the group members to introduce themselves, if appropriate.
- Explain 'housekeeping' arrangements, such as meal times, breaks, where facilities are, etc.

2   What is violent behaviour?

- Using a simple exercise, such as a brainstorm, get the group to identify behaviour that is violent. Record these on the flipchart.
- Explain that the term 'violence' is being used to describe a wide range

of behaviour (rather than using other words, such as 'aggression', 'abusive behaviour', 'rudeness', 'harassment') of the physical and non-physical type (see Handout 2).

- Ask the group if they can now add to the original list of violent behaviour – help them, if necessary.
- Using the working definitions of violence (see Chapter 4 and Handout 1), if you wish, ensure that the group has a shared understanding of behaviour that constitutes violence, and its effects (see Handout 4).

BREAK – 15 mins

3 Causes and signs of danger

- Causes of violence – lead a group discussion, having posed the question 'Why do people become violent?' The discussion should identify a range of possible causes, from drunkenness and drug-taking to frustration or anger because of perceived poor service, or 'You've picked on my son.'
- Identify the most likely causes of violence in the workplace(s) of group members.
- Signs of danger – explain to the group that both verbal and non-verbal communication can signal impending violence (see Chapter 16). Verbal threats or suggestions of violence are readily recognized. However, verbal signals are generally much rarer than non-verbal, so recognizing non-verbal signs of danger is important.
- Get the group to identify non-verbal signs of danger – this is often most effectively done by asking volunteers to demonstrate anger or frustration by giving them a short role-play exercise.
- Review the role-play (or any other activity you may have used), and either write up a list of the behaviour identified as danger signs, provide the group with a prepared handout based on Chapter 16 or use Handout 6.

4 What to do when faced with violence

- Distinguish between physical and non-physical violence (see Handout 2), and explain that after lunch, they will learn one method that can help in coping with non-physical violence.
- Physical violence – explain that the options when facing physical attack are:
  - getting away;
  - fighting back – fighting free;
  - defusing the situation.

Ask the group how they would get away, fight back or try to defuse the situation. For each response, use the text (see Chapter 17, pp. 127–39) to explain good safe practice and to explain why some of the ideas they may have are actually likely to put them at greater risk.

- Develop with the group (or use a prepared handout) a list of key points to remember in the event of physical attack.
- Someone is likely to raise the issue of self-defence; ensure they are clear about the pros and cons of learning and attempting to use self-defence.

BREAK FOR LUNCH – 1 hour

5   The control trilogy

- Introduce the control trilogy (see Chapter 17) as a useful method for helping to deal with non-physical violence; make sure the group remember they do not have to try to cope if it is safer not to do so, and that they are clear that the control trilogy should not be assumed to always be appropriate or successful.
- Using the text and handouts you prepare from it, go through each of the stages – calming, reaching and controlling – explaining its purpose, what it involves, answering questions, discussing points, etc.
- Give the group time to read the material you have provided and clarify the points.
- Set up a practice exercise using role-play outlines you have prepared that are relevant in the group's working environment, and allow them to practise the stages of the control trilogy.

Trio exercises work well for this kind of practice, with three roles: the violent person, the subject, and an observer. Each of the group members (A, B and C) gets the chance to play each role. Table T3.1 shows how it works.

Table T3.1   Control trilogy – trio exercise

	Violent person	Subject	Observer
Time period 1	A	B	C
Time period 2	C	A	B
Time period 3	B	C	A

You need to make clear there are three time periods, and they need to be about 20 minutes each. You need to brief the observers on what to look for (changes in behaviour, what worked or did not, etc.).

- Review the exercise, picking out key learning points, what the group felt about the method, what worked and did not work, how and in what circumstances the group feel they could or would use the method.

BREAK – 15 mins

6   Action plans

- Ask the group to individually prepare an action plan, identifying what they will do to implement what they have learnt, for example:
  - What will they do differently?
  - How will they use what they have learnt to help them recognize danger and cope with possibly violent people?
  - What will they avoid doing?
- With the whole group – or those who wish to do so – work out a timetable for further practice of the control trilogy.

7   Summary/evaluation

- Summarize the key learning points from the day, either verbally or written up on an overhead projector, flipchart or handout.
- Using an evaluation exercise questionnaire, ask the group to identify, for example, what has been:
  - most useful/least useful;
  - well done/not so well done;
  - most enjoyable/least enjoyable;
  - most relevant/least relevant;

and what they will:

  - use at work/not use;
  - use in their personal life/not use;

and what they would have liked:

  - more of/less of;
  - to include/to exclude.

- Explain any further evaluation process that you wish to conduct with them.

Task 4 Communication skills

Aim

To enable learners to develop communication skills that will help them avoid or cope with violent situations.

Objectives

At the end of the programme, learners will be able to:

- describe how self-awareness and the awareness of others contributes to effective communication;
- explain what is meant by 'body language' (see Chapter 16), and its importance in communication;
- explain what is meant by 'assertiveness' (see Chapter 18 and Hand-out 8);
- demonstrate assertive communication.

Time

One day.

Target groups

All staff, but particularly those who regularly deal with the public, parents, children and other colleagues, including senior colleagues.

Resources

Overhead projector and/or flipchart and pens, any prepared materials and handouts (e.g. comparisons of types of behaviour, list of 'rights'; (see Chapter 18, pp. 141–53).

Environment

A room large enough for the whole group to split into smaller groups for practice, or preferably, separate rooms or further space for practice sessions.

Timetable

1 Introduction	30 mins
2 Non-verbal communication	1¼ hours
BREAK	15 mins
3 Assertiveness – introduction	1¼ hours
LUNCH	1 hour
4 Assertiveness – practice	2¼ hours (includes break taken as appropriate)
5 Action plan	15 mins
6 Summary/evaluation	30 mins

Contents

1   Introduction

- Introduce yourself.
- Use a brief exercise to enable the participants to introduce themselves.
- Introduce the programme, using the aims and objectives to describe the content and outcomes.
- Explain any 'housekeeping' arrangements, such as break times, finish time, where facilities, including fire exits, are located, etc.
- Make clear to the group that there are benefits of effective communication in dealing with difficult or potentially dangerous situations, and risks in not paying attention to what and how we communicate.

2   Non-verbal communication

- Explain the importance of non-verbal communication, or body language, in communication as a whole, and why it is important to understand it in order to avoid or cope with difficult or violent situations.
- Discuss with the group the possible effects of impressions and stereotypes we all have. Ask them for examples from their own experience to show both the risks and possible advantages of these.
- For each of the elements of body language identified in Chapter 16 (dress, listening), select a method of conveying to the group its importance and effects in non-verbal communication. For example:
  - in relation to dress, you could show them pictures and ask them about the wearer of the clothes;
  - for facial expression or body posture, you could ask volunteers to demonstrate (as in charades) feelings to the group;
  - for voice, you could ask several people to say the same thing in different ways;
  - for listening, you could demonstrate the difference between active listening and just 'being there'.
- Sum up the session by asking the whole group to complete a list of:
  - positive non-verbal communication they could adopt;
  - non-verbal 'danger' signals they will look out for.

BREAK – 15 mins

3   Assertiveness – introduction

- Explain that assertive behaviour is a learned 'positive' behaviour, and that it involves recognizing and respecting the rights, feelings, needs and opinions of yourself and others. It is not about getting your own way all the time .
- For each of the behaviour types in Chapter 18 and Handout 7 (aggressive, passive, manipulative and assertive), identify with the group:
  - what each behaviour is characterized by;
  - the effects of the behaviour on others.

You could ask the whole group to identify characteristics and effects initially, and then add to it. You could create four sub-groups and ask each of them to take one of the behaviours, identify the characteristics and effects, and feed their results back to the whole group, where everyone could add to their work; or each sub-group could consider all four behaviour types and then compare results.

- Summarize the key points that distinguish assertive behaviour as an effective and positive form of communication.

BREAK FOR LUNCH – 1 hour

4   Assertiveness – practice

- Explain the rights of individuals and the importance of remembering that we and others have the same rights; also why remembering our rights and those of others is important (see Chapter 18, pp. 141–53).
- For each of the areas of communication (from making requests to feedback, see Chapter 18, pp. 141–53), or those most relevant to the group, explain how to communicate assertively in each area, or ask them for their ideas of assertive approaches and add to them through discussion in the group.
- In order to practise assertive communication, you could provide role-play outlines for the group to work through, or you could ask them for examples of real-life situations from the work setting that they could practise on.
- Once the group has had the opportunity to practise, review with them what they have found difficult or easy, and identify what are the key points of assertive communication that must be remembered.

5   Action plan

Ask each group member to prepare an action plan for themselves, outlining what action they will take to implement their learning about:

- non-verbal communication;
- assertive communication.

They may then explain their plan to another group member or a sub-group, who could help clarify or expand their plan.

With the whole group (or those who wish), agree a timetable for further practice of assertive communication.

6   Summary/evaluation

- Summarize the main learning points from the day, either verbally or as a prepared written list – or ask the group to contribute to a list you compile together, if time permits.
- Conduct an evaluation, using a form or group exercise that will provide information about what the group perceived as:

- of greatest value;
- most useful to them at work;
- should be kept/should be dropped;
- most/least interesting or enjoyable;
- well done/not so well done;
- most/least difficult.

● Explain any further or follow-up evaluation you plan to conduct.

Task 5 Developing policy and procedures

Aim

To encourage and enable managers (and others involved) to develop policies and procedures to protect employees from violence.

Objectives

At the end of the programme, the learners will be able to:

- develop a draft definition of violence relevant in their workplace;
- identify the duties of employers and employees in respect of safety from violence at work;
- identify areas of potential risk within their own organization;
- describe the elements of a policy on violence at work;
- draft a policy for the organization;
- develop procedures necessary to implement the policy.

Time

Two days.

Target groups

Policy-makers, managers or others involved in the development of the policy on violence: for example, teaching and support staff of all kinds, advisory and personnel staff, representatives on health and safety committees, management and employees.

Resources

Flipchart, pens and/or overhead projector, handouts and other prepared materials.

Environment

A room large enough to allow the whole group to work comfortably, and space or syndicate rooms for sub-groups. Where managers and policy-makers are involved, it is as well to be away from the workplace to avoid interruptions.

Timetable

Day 1

1	Introduction	1 hour
2	Defining violence at work	1 hour
BREAK		30 mins
3	Duties of employers	1½ hours
BREAK FOR LUNCH		1 hour
4	Identifying risks at work	2 hours
BREAK		15 mins
5	Summary/looking forward	45 mins

Day 2

1	Introduction	15 mins
2	Policy development	3½ hours (includes 30 mins break taken as appropriate)
2	Policy development (continued)	
BREAK FOR LUNCH		1 hour
3	Developing procedures	1½ hours
BREAK		15 mins
4	Action plans	45 mins
5	Summary/evaluation	45 mins

Contents

Day 1

1   Introduction

- Introduce yourself.
- Ask the participants to introduce themselves – they will almost certainly know each others' names and roles, as they are from the same organization, so design an activity to get them to know each other better and start working together.
- Explain any 'housekeeping' arrangements, such as start and finish times, break times, location of facilities including fire exits, etc.
- Using the aims and objectives, explain the purpose, content and outcomes of the programme, stressing the practical outcomes for their organization.
- Select key research findings and other information from the text (see Chapter 4) to demonstrate that there is a growing body of evidence that confirms that violence at work is a problem, as well as that the problem is on the increase.

2   Defining violence at work

- Explain to the group what a working definition of 'violence' is, its purpose, and why it is important (see Chapter 4 and Handout 1).
- Develop a group definition (draft organizational definition), either by:
  - setting sub-groups the task of coming up with a definition, and then discussing these in the whole group to come to a group definition. You can then compare with the example in the text and refine if necessary;

  or

  - showing the group the example working definitions, discuss these and work as a whole group towards a definition that meets their needs and those of their organization.

BREAK – 15 mins

3   Duties of employers and employees

- Pose the group (or sub-groups) the following questions (see Chapter 5 and Handout 3):

-   What are the duties of employers in relation to the safety of staff from violence?
-   What are the costs of not fulfilling the duties (see Handout 4)?

Either record the responses of the whole group, or get each sub-group to record their answers. If you work with sub-groups, ask them to feed back their answers to the whole group.

●   Using prepared overhead projector slides, a flipchart or a handout from the text, compare the groups' answers to the information in the text:

-   How accurate were they?
-   Did they realize the extent of the duties upon employers and employees?
-   Were they aware of the action that could be taken against them as employers/individuals?
-   Did they identify the possible costs to individuals and the organization of not tackling problems of violence to staff?

Ask the group to identify where they feel they do and do not fulfil their duties.

BREAK FOR LUNCH – 1 hour

4   Identifying risks at work

●   Remind the group of what they said before lunch about how far they believe they do or do not fulfil their duties as employers or employees.
●   Can they be sure, if there has been no systematic or thorough investigation?

-   Would other employees generally share their view?

●   Explain the types of job that have associated risks, using the Health and Safety Executive's categories (in Handout 9).

-   How many of the organization's activities (see Chapter 6) carry risks?
-   What other activities does the organization undertake that may have associated risks?

●   Where to investigate

-   Explain the idea of an audit as a means of investigating risks (see Chapter 6).
-   Select a number of areas worth investigating relevant to the particular organization, and ask the group members to identify questions or concerns about these areas they would want to investigate.

Discuss the questions and concerns they identify, adding to or amending their lists from the text (see Chapter 6) as appropriate, or from the ideas of the rest of the group.

- How to investigate? Discuss with the group the questions posed in the text:

   - What information do you want?
   - What form of information do you want?
   - How much information should you collect?
   - Who should conduct the investigation?

It is important that they are able to consider these questions before getting into the detail of individual methods.

- For each of the methods of collecting information described in the text (see Chapter 6 and Handout 10):

   - describe it briefly, if necessary;
   - ask for views of the advantages and disadvantages of using the method, adding information as required;
   - ask the group to say which methods they believe would work best for them, and why;
   - ask if they have any other ideas or methods that may work well in the organization or part of it.

BREAK – 15 mins

5   Summary/looking forward

- Summarize the key learning points from today's sessions, either for the group or with them.
- Outline the timetable for tomorrow, explaining how the work from today links to the work on developing policy and procedure.

Day 2

1   Introduction

Introduce the programme for the day, explaining that the purpose of the morning's activities is to produce a draft policy for the organization, and the afternoon will focus on developing outline procedures necessary to support the policy. In both these activities, they will be drawing on learning from Day 1.

2   Policy development

As this is a long session, it is advisable to take a 30-minute break when you feel the group needs it.

- Ensure that the group is clear what is meant by a policy, and what its purposes are.
- Using the headings from the text (see Chapter 7 and Handout 11), identify the areas normally covered by a policy, and briefly, what each of these covers. These areas may or may not suit the particular organization's requirements, so may need to be changed – one or more left out and/or others added. Agree with the group the areas their draft policy will cover.
- The whole group could attempt to draft the whole policy, but this may prove very difficult. A more effective approach could be to set up three or four sub-groups, each of which takes responsibility for producing a first draft of a number of the policy areas.
- Once the sub-groups have completed drafts of their areas of the policy, they return to the whole group. In the whole group, each policy area, starting at the beginning, can then be taken in turn and discussed, amended, added to or otherwise developed until a final draft is agreed.
- Sub-groups can then write up the final draft of the policy areas they are responsible for.
- Discuss and agree with the group the process for taking the draft policy forward in the organization, for example:

  - Who will take responsibility for typing, copying, circulating the draft, and so on?
  - Who needs to see the draft?
  - What sort of consultation process is necessary?
  - What will be the timescale?
  - Who will be responsible for overseeing policy development from here on?

BREAK FOR LUNCH – 1 hour

3   Developing procedures

- The group yesterday identified possible risks at work and have now drafted a policy. The next step is to consider the procedures required to implement the policy and tackle the potential risks of violence they have identified. They will probably need more information (from an investigation of some sort) in order to be precise about procedures; here, they are developing proposals for the procedures they believe are likely to be required.

- Using the examples of the sorts of procedure likely to be required, ask the group to identify where they believe the organization needs:

  - to develop new procedures;
  - to change existing procedures;
  - to abandon current procedures.

  Record their responses.

- Once you have a list of their responses, help the group to prioritize the needs by identifying, for example:

  - areas of greatest risk that require urgent attention;
  - actions that can be taken immediately to deal with obvious risks;
  - cost-effective action to which there will be no resistance;
  - changes that may meet with resistance for some reason and will require consultation with, or the persuasion of, others;
  - areas where no action can be taken without further investigation.

- Discuss and agree with the group how their proposals can or will be used:

  - Who will be responsible for writing them up/presenting them?
  - To whom should they go?
  - Should they accompany the draft policy?
  - Should they be kept to a later stage of the policy development process?

BREAK – 15 mins

4 Action plans

- Individuals draw up their own action plan, identifying:

  - action they have agreed to take on behalf of the group to further its work on this programme;
  - action they will take immediately in their role to minimize the risk of violence to themselves and others;
  - action they will take individually to further support the development of policy and procedures;
  - action they will take to further develop their own knowledge and skills in relation to combating violence at work;
  - timescales for their actions;
  - help or support they require.

- In pairs, trios or small groups, each person takes it in turn to explain their action plan; others can help them, for example by adding to the plan, clarifying points, offering support or agreeing to review their progress with them at a later stage.

5   Summary/evaluation

- Summarize the key learning points from the various sessions in the programme with the group (or for them), verbally or as written notes.
- Using a form or group exercise, evaluate the programme, including aspects such as:

  - content – appropriateness; relevance; depth; variety;
  - style – participation/listening; active/inactive;
  - time – length of programme; duration of sessions; timing of breaks;
  - materials – quantity; quality; range;
  - trainers – approach; confidence with subject; presentation;
  - venue – facilities; comfort; access; refreshments.

Task 6 Practical steps to safety

This programme is designed for particular groups of staff with particular needs because of the risks they face – for example, reception staff, travelling staff such as advisers, inspectors, educational welfare officers, youth leaders, teachers between sites, staff who work in others' homes or premises, staff who handle money, and so on. The first part of the programme is common, while the second part of the programme differs, depending upon the group being trained.

Aim

To provide participants with practical knowledge of steps they can take to keep safe.

Objectives

At the end of the programme, the learners will be able to:

- identify potential areas of risk in their work;
- describe practical steps they can take to keep safe in the course of their work;
- develop an action plan describing the steps they will take:
  - to change the way they work;
  - to bring about changes in procedures to ensure safety;
  - to obtain help, support and resources they need.

Time

One day.

Resources

Overhead projector, flipchart and pens, prepared materials and handouts.

Environment

A room large enough to allow space for sub-groups to work, or separate syndicate rooms.

Timetable

1 Introduction	30 mins
2 Violence at work and its effects	30 mins
3 The risks of violence	1 hour
BREAK	15 mins
4 Practical session 1	1½ hours
BREAK FOR LUNCH	1 hour
5 Practical session 2	2 hours
BREAK	15 mins
6 Action plan	30 mins
7 Summary/evaluation	30 mins

Contents

1   Introduction

- Introduce yourself.
- Ask participants to introduce themselves, using a name game or similar warm-up exercise.
- Explain the content and outcomes of the programme, using the aims and objectives.

2   Violence at work and its effects

- Ask the group what behaviour they would describe as violence at work, including any examples from their experience.
- Show the group the working definitions of violence at work from the text (see Chapter 4 and Handout 1) and discuss them, for example:
  - whether or not they agree with them;
  - if they are wider definitions than they expected;
  - if they cover the areas of behaviour and effects the group think they should.
- Agree a working definition with the group, so that everyone is clear about the basis from which the group is working.

3   The risks of violence

- Using the research material in the text (see Chapters 2 and 3), select examples to illustrate the increasing recognition of violence at work as a problem. Discuss with the group whether they agree with the research findings or not, and why they think violence may be on the increase.
- Explain, using figures cited in the text (see Chapters 2 and 3), the risks of crime. Ask the group if the statistics are what they expected, or very different. Ask if they feel they are at risk from crime and, if so, why.

BREAK

4 and 5   Practical sessions 1 and 2

These sessions should be designed to meet the needs of the particular group and use the material appropriate to the areas of activity and tasks that the group identifies. (Break for lunch between sessions.)

- Work with the group through the activities and tasks they perform, and the way they perform them, to identify the risks they face in relation to each.
- Ask the group for ideas or suggestions as to how they could do their jobs more safely and what support, equipment, resources and so on they need in order to do so. Add to their ideas using prepared materials.
- Depending upon the number of areas of activity or tasks the group identifies, set up sub-groups, and ask each group to develop good practice guidelines for one or more of the activities or tasks identified.

- Feed back the good practice guidelines to the whole group, adding to them or amending them as the group members contribute their ideas and observations.

BREAK – 15 mins

6   Action plan

- Each individual should identify in their action plans:
  - tasks or activities they will perform differently to minimize any risks to them;
  - support, help, equipment, and so on, they will try to obtain in order to make their jobs safer;
  - how they will try to bring about any changes in procedure/practice to minimize the risk of violence at work;
  - further information, advice or training they feel they need, and how they plan to go about obtaining what they need.

  Ask the group members to try to build in timescales, and to find others in the group to support them in achieving their action plan and/or help them assess their progress at an agreed point.

7   Summary/evaluation

- Summarise the key learning points from each of the sessions during the day for the group, or ask the group or sub-groups to develop a summary of the sessions for discussion and add to it in the whole group.
- Evaluate the programme to obtain immediate reactions, such as:
  - how relevant the group felt it was;
  - whether it was practical enough;
  - what more they would have liked;
  - what they would keep the same or change.

- Explain to the group when and how any future evaluation of the programme will take place.

Appendix A

Sample handouts

These handouts can be prepared in advance of training sessions, for distribution to participants. They can also be used to prepare transparencies for use with overhead projectors.

Handout 1: Definitions of violence

- 'Any incident in which an employee is abused, threatened or assaulted by a member of the public in circumstances arising out of the course of his or her employment' (Health and Safety Executive's working definition of violence, 1988)
- 'The application of force, severe threat or serious abuse by members of the public towards people arising out of the course of their work whether or not they are on duty. This includes severe verbal abuse or threat where this is judged likely to turn into actual violence; serious or persistent harassment (including racial or sexual harassment); threat with a weapon; major or minor injuries; fatalities' (Department of Health and Social Security Advisory Committee on Violence to Staff, 1988)
- 'Behaviour which produces damaging or hurtful effects, physically or emotionally, on people' (Association of Directors of Social Services, 1987)

Handout 2: Examples of violence

Physical violence

- assault causing death;
- assault causing serious physical injury;
- minor injuries;
- kicking;
- biting;
- punching;
- use of weapons;
- use of missiles;
- spitting;
- scratching;
- sexual assault;
- deliberate self-harm.

Non-physical violence

- verbal abuse;
- racial or sexual abuse;
- threats – with or without weapons;
- physical posturing;
- threatening gestures;
- abusive phone calls;
- threatening use of dogs;
- harassment in all forms;
- swearing;
- shouting;
- name-calling;
- bullying;
- insults;
- innuendo;
- deliberate silence.

Handout 3: Employer's duties (Health and Safety at Work Act, 1974)

The general obligation: 'it shall be the duty of every employer to ensure so far as is reasonably practicable, the health, safety and welfare of all his employees'. The matters to which that duty extends include:

- 'The provision and maintenance of plant and systems of work that are, so far as is reasonably practicable, safe and without risk to health'
- 'The provision of such information, instruction, training and supervision as is necessary to ensure, so far as is reasonably practicable, the health and safety at work of his employees'
- 'The provision and maintenance of a working environment for his employees that is, so far as is reasonably practicable, safe and without risk to health'

In addition, there is an obligation to draw up and publish written safety policies to include these matters. Apart from the obligations under the Health and Safety at Work Act, there are other obligations on an employer arising from:

- the employer's duty of care under Common Law for the safety of his employees;
- the employer's duty under any nationally negotiated agreements;
- the employer's duty not to dismiss employees unfairly. Employees have resigned in some situations and successfully alleged constructive unfair dismissal because the employer failed to provide reasonable precautions for the employee's safety, thus establishing a precedent.

Handout 4: Effects of violence on staff

Any form of violence, whether or not it results in some sort of physical injury, can have serious effects on the workforce, including:

- high levels of anxiety;
- stress-related illness;
- absenteeism and the need to cover for staff;
- low morale;
- high levels of staff turnover;
- low productivity;
- little job satisfaction;
- low employee involvement;
- industrial action or poor industrial relations;
- difficulty in recruiting and retaining staff.

Handout 5: Developing an action plan

- Find out if there is a problem.
- Record all incidents.
- Classify all incidents.
- Search for preventive measures.
- Decide what to do.
- Put measures into practice.
- Check that measures work.

Handout 6: Signs of danger

In dealing with others, watch for the following:

- raised voice, rapid speech and gabbling, as this signals rising tension;
- changes in tone and pitch as the conversation progresses that may suggest anger, frustration or impending violent behaviour;
- slow, menacing tones that, despite the words themselves, demonstrate that the speaker is angry and likely to erupt into violent behaviour.

Handout 7: Some characteristics of aggressive, manipulative and passive behaviour

AGGRESSIVE	MANIPULATIVE	PASSIVE
Recognizing own rights only	Avoiding direct approach	Acting as a 'doormat'
Forceful expressions of opinion	Covert expressions of views	Failure to express views
Need to prove superiority	Skills at deceiving	Decision-making problems
Giving orders rather than requests	Need to be in control	Blaming others
Blaming others	Not trusting self or others	Resignation
Putting people down	Denial of feelings	Giving in
Not listening to others	Insincerity	Saying 'yes' – meaning 'no'
Competitiveness	Making veiled threats	Complaining behind the scenes
Verbal abuse, insults	Using guilt as a weapon	Not knowing own boundaries
Over-reacting	Sabotage behind the scenes	
Egocentricity	Using derogatory language	
Threats	Talking behind people's backs	

Handout 8: Characteristics of assertive behaviour

Assertive behaviour is characterized by:

- self-respect and self-esteem;
- respect for others;
- recognition of your own and others' rights;
- acceptance of your own positive and negative qualities and those of others;
- acknowledging your own responsibility for your choices and actions;
- recognizing your own needs, wants and feelings, being able to express them, and allowing others to do the same;
- listening to others;
- being able to ask for your own needs to be met and risk refusal;
- accepting that you do not always get what you want; feeling rejection, but not being destroyed by it;
- open and honest interaction with others;
- knowing your own limits; ability to say 'no' and respect others' limits or boundaries;
- giving feedback or constructive criticism when it is due, accepting it of yourself if valid, or rejecting it if it is not.

Handout 9:   Where workers are at risk

The Health and Safety Executive breaks high-risk jobs into the following categories:

- Giving a service: benefits office, housing department;
- Caring: nurses, social workers, community care staff;
- Education: teachers, support staff;
- Money transactions: post offices, banks, shops, building societies, bus drivers/conductors;
- Delivery/collection: milk delivery, postal services, rent collection;
- Controlling: reception staff, security staff, traffic wardens;
- Inspecting: building inspectors, planning officers.

Handout 10: Methods for information collection

Methods of collecting information include the use of questionnaires, observation, structured interviews, working groups and the use of external consultants.

Other methods which have proved effective include:

- suggestion boxes;
- use of team meetings with heads of department, supervisors or managers;
- staff meetings or departmental meetings;
- asking people to write in with views, ideas, problems, opinions, and so on;
- open forums with safety or personnel staff;
- visits to other workplaces to observe different practices.

Handout 11: Areas covered by a policy on violence at work

- Policy title
- The purpose (or aim or objective)
- Definition
- The philosophy
- Whom the policy covers
- What the employer is committed to do
- What is required of individuals
- Performance measures
- Evaluation/review

Appendix B

Crimestoppers

Crimestoppers Trust

What is Crimestoppers?

Crimestoppers is a national crime information collection scheme which enables the public to give information anonymously using the Crimestoppers freephone number 0800 555 111. It operates 24 hours a day every day of the year.

When did Crimestoppers begin in the UK?

Crimestoppers began in London in January 1988 following many months of research and discussion by the Home Office and the police. No government funding was available and the business community was approached. Michael Ashcroft, Chairman of ADT, agreed to establish a trust fund which was registered as a charity. The charity was then known as Community Action Trust. As Crimestoppers became increasingly successful, the decision was made to change to a new, more meaningful, name. The charity became Crimestoppers Trust on 23 June 1995.

How does Crimestoppers operate?

Crimestoppers Trust acts as a national co-ordinating agency for regional Crimestoppers schemes throughout the UK. Within each Crimestoppers region (there are over twenty) a local board made up of businessmen, councillors and others of standing within the community, promotes the scheme. They provide the link between the police, the media and the community and promote the 0800 500 111 national freephone telephone number.

Who is Crimestoppers aimed at?

Crimestoppers is aimed at everyone who has information on crime but is frightened or unwilling for any reason to approach the police directly. The guaranteed anonymity of Crimestoppers removes any fear of retribution or compromise.

Is Crimestoppers successful?

Yes, and it becomes increasingly more so each year. Every year has been a record year for Crimestoppers. In the past two years alone Crimestoppers has been involved in the arrest and charge of 6,298 people and has helped recover over £10.8 million worth of stolen goods.

Who pays for all of this?

Crimestoppers is not funded by the government. It relies entirely on donations and grants from business, trusts and the public, and, as the scheme becomes more successful, the need for funds increases each year.

In 1976 in Albuquerque USA, when the local police were having no success in their search for perpetrators of a series of armed robberies, a young man working at a petrol station in town was shot and killed. The detective investigating the crimes believed they had been committed by local people and that someone must know who they were but was unwilling to talk to the police. After six weeks of getting nowhere he devised the idea of a telephone 'hotline' for people to pass on information anonymously. He persuaded local businessmen to finance the scheme and the local television station to publicize it. Within 72 hours of the TV broadcast the 'hotline' produced information which led to the arrest of two people who were later convicted of the murder. At the same time many other crimes were solved as a result of calls to the 'hotline'. Crimestoppers had begun.

Appendix C

Record of risk assessment form

Record of risk assessment

Name of school ....

Hazard assessed ....

Location .... Date of assessment ....

Description of risk (including likely persons involved)

Risk significance

Not significant ....

Low ....

Moderate ....

High ....

Very high ....

Action required

Immediate ....

Short term ....

Long term ....

Action to be taken by (name) .... Review date ....

Assessment undertaken by (responsible person) ....

Appendix D

Violent incident report form

Incident report form: violence and aggression to staff

(Includes physical violence, aggression, verbal abuse, sexual or racial abuse, intentional damage to personal property.)

Managers of staff who have been victims of violence or aggression should complete this form as fully as possible. It will help us to understand the problems staff face in their work and to see ways to reduce the risk of future incidents. Please use continuation sheet if necessary.

Date of incident	Day of week	Time

1 Employee – personal details of person assaulted

Name .... Work address ....

Job/Position ....

Dept/Section .... Age .... Gender ....

What work was being done when incident started? ....

....

2 Details of assailant(s) if known   3 Witness(es) if any

Name(s) ....   Name(s) ....

Address(es) ....   Address(es) ....

Age(s) approx. ....

Gender ....

Description ....

Relationship between employee and assailant, if any ....

....

4   Details of incident

   a) Type of assault (including any injury suffered, treatment received, time off
      work, etc.)

   b) Location of incident (attach sketch if appropriate)

   c) Other details: please describe incident, including relevant events leading up
      to it, relevant details of assailant not given above, if a weapon was involved,
      members of staff present.

   ....

   ....

5   Outcome (e.g. whether police called, what happened after the incident, any legal
    action)

   ....

   ....

6   Other information (to be completed as appropriate)

   a) Possible contributory factors ....

      ....

   b) Is assailant known to have been involved in any previous incidents?   YES/NO

   c) Give date and brief details of (b) if known ....

      ....

      ....

   d) Had any measures been taken to try to prevent an incident of this type
      occurring? If so, what? How did they fall short? How could they be improved?

      ....

      ....

      ....

e) Even if no measures had been taken beforehand, in your view could action now be taken? If so what and has it been taken? ....

....

....

....

....

f) Any other relevant information ....

....

....

Signed .... Date ....

Position .... Please return as soon as possible to:

....

Analysis of reports

When a violent incident reporting system is set up, arrangements need to be made to analyse the data produced so that it can be used effectively in designing preventive strategies. There will be a number of different ways that information on violence can be classified to give a picture of problem areas; ESAC suggests the following break-downs may be helpful.

		No. of reports
Personnel involved e.g.	Head/deputy	
	Teacher	
	Residential social worker	
	Supervisor	
	Secretary/clerk	
	Caretaker	
	Youth worker	
	Education welfare officer	
	Nursery nurse	
	Parent helper	
	Classroom/nursery assistant	
	Educational psychologist	

		No. of reports
Type of establishment e.g.	Secondary school	
	Middle school	
	Primary school	
	Special school	
	College	
	Residential hostel	
	Youth club	
	Field centre	
	Pupil's home	

		No. of reports
Assailants	Pupil/student	
	Parent	
	Intruders	
	Other	

		No. of reports
Type of incident	*Physical*	

Assaults while disciplining pupils
    (a)   Physically restraining a pupil
    (b)   intervening in a fight
    (c)   dealing with a disobedient pupil
    (d)   excluding a pupil from the classroom
    (e)   apparently unprovoked
    (f)   other
Assaults from a distance
    (a)   hit by a missile
Assaults by pupils' families
    (a)   on teachers
    (b)   on other employees
    (c)   on contractors' staff on site
Assaults from intruders on site

Verbal
Written
Other types

An annual report on the data will help identify:

(a)   changes in the number of incidents recorded over time (to indicate trends and help highlight whether prevention programmes are being successful);
(b)   changes in number of incidents for particular categories of staff;
(c)   increases in number or severity of particular incidents (to identify areas where further work is a priority).

Reprinted from the Education Service Advisory Committee (1990) *Violence to Staff in the Education Sector*, with kind permission of the HSE and HMSO.

Appendix E

Bullying in the workplace

Bullying in the workplace

Bullying used to be considered a problem confined to pupils. However, since the incidence of bullying within the workplace was highlighted through the campaign by the indefatigable Andrea Adams, before her untimely death in 1995, it has been recognized as a very real problem. Bullying within the educational sector workplace was particularly highlighted at a meeting in the House of Lords on the subject in March 1996.

The Police Federation have been one of the foremost agencies in putting together guidance for staff on this subject. We are grateful to them for allowing us to reprint their ideas which may help schools, colleges and other educational establishments to draw up similar papers.

Definition

Workplace bullying constitutes unwanted, offensive, humiliating, undermining behaviour towards an individual or groups of employees. Such persistently malicious attacks on personal or professional performance are typically unpredictable, irrational and often unfair. This abuse of power or position can cause such chronic stress and anxiety that people gradually lose belief in themselves, suffering physical ill health and mental distress as a result.

Bullying in the workplace has only recently come to prominence. Workplace bullying affects working conditions, health and safety, domestic life and the right of all to equal opportunity and treatment.

Workplace bullying is a separate issue from sexual or racial harassment. Bullies can be regarded as persons who use their position or power to coerce others by fear or persecution, or oppress them by force or threat.

Bullying is a gradual wearing down process that makes individuals feel demeaned and inadequate, that they can never get anything right, and that they are hopeless, not only within their work environment but also in their domestic life.

In many instances, bullying can be very difficult to detect. It often takes place where there are no witnesses. It can be subtle and devious, and it is difficult for those on the receiving end to confront their perpetrator.

The legal position

The Department of Trade and Industry, which is responsible for employment protection legislation, states:

> Employers are encouraged to treat their employees with consideration, and bullying and intimidation of employees by their managers is to be deplored. In some circumstances it may indeed be an offence under the Criminal Justice and Public Order Act 1994.
>
> Employers also have a general duty under health and safety legislation to protect their employees against ill-health caused by work, and this duty extends to stress related ill-health which might be caused by persistent bullying at work.
>
> Victims of bullying may also be able to pursue other means of redress through unfair dismissal or discrimination legislation.

So far, the Health and Safety Commission have not accepted that this subject comes under their remit of 'violence at work', or under their stress directorate.

However, The Suzy Lamplugh Trust does feel that it falls within the remit of 'personal safety', and certainly, the implementation of a policy statement on bullying can prove very helpful in establishing principles and practices which help to improve the ethos, efficiency and effectiveness in the service provided to the pupils and public as a whole.

What constitutes bullying within the workplace?

- offensive treatment through vindictive, cruel, malicious or humiliating attempts to undermine an individual employee or groups of employees;
- persistently negative attacks on personal and professional performance, which are typically unpredictable, irrational and often unseen;

This abuse of power or position can cause chronic stress and anxiety to the extent that an employee gradually loses belief in themselves, suffering physical ill health and mental distress.

Forms of bullying

- persistent criticism;
- setting objectives with impossible deadlines, or tasks which are unachievable in the time allowed;
- ignoring or excluding an individual by talking only to a third party to isolate another; freezing people out;
- withholding information;
- removing areas of responsibility, and giving people menial or trivial tasks to do instead;

- constantly undervaluing effort;
- spreading malicious rumours;
- blocking leave or training applications for no reason;
- taking credit for other people's ideas.

Identifying a bully

A bully within the work environment is a person who:

- is likely to have Jekyll and Hyde characteristics;
- insists their method of working is always right;
- tells people what needs to be done, then keeps changing the instructions, perhaps in the hope people will make mistakes;
- shouts at people in order to get things done;
- persistently picks on, criticizes and humiliates people in front of others;
- gives people tasks that he/she knows they are incapable of achieving;
- blames everyone but themselves when things go wrong.

Why are people bullied?

A bully will attack certain individuals for a number of reasons, the most prevalent being:

- popularity among colleagues;
- success;
- achievement;
- efficiency;
- organizational expertise;
- superior social skills.

Detecting bullying

Supervisory and senior management can detect bullying by recognizing certain changes within the working environment, such as:

- high turnover;
- high levels of absenteeism;
- regular or prolonged sickness absence;
- low morale;
- loss of initiative;
- staff looking tense or troubled.

Emotional and physical symptoms linked to bullying

People who are being bullied often suffer from a number of stress-related symptoms, such as:

Emotional

- loss of confidence;
- loss of self-esteem;
- lack of motivation;
- irritability/aggression;
- acute anxiety;
- panic attacks;
- anger/murderous feelings;
- depression;
- suicidal thoughts.

Physical

- sleeplessness;
- nausea;
- sweating/shaking;
- palpitations;
- lethargy;
- skin complaints;
- backache;
- stomach/bowel problems;
- migraine/severe headaches.

Action to be taken if you are being bullied

- You may be able to recognize the early symptoms of bullying and confront the perpetrator by telling them you are not prepared to tolerate their behaviour and you want it to stop.
- If you do not, or are unable to, confront the bully, keep a written record (including dates and details) of all the attacks and incidents, including slurs on your character, competence and standard of work. Follow this up by sending memos to the perpetrator regarding their behaviour and claims.
- Talk about the bullying you are experiencing with your colleagues, and if it is happening to them join together, take firm, positive action, and make a collective complaint.
- If the bullying continues, collate all the evidence you have gathered and present it either to your immediate line supervisor, senior personnel officer, equal opportunities officer or union representative. They will be able to advise you on what to do next.

Sources of help and advice

ACAS
Head Office
Brandon House
180 Borough High Street
London
SE1 1LW

Tel: 0171 210 3000, or your local ACAS office

British Association for Counselling
1 Regent Place
Rugby
Warwickshire
CV21 2PJ

Tel: 01788 550 899 (administration) 01788 578 328 (information)

Commission for Racial Equality
Head Office
Elliot House
10–12 Allington Street
London
SW1E 5EH

Tel: 0171 828 7022

Equal Opportunities Commission
Head Office
Overseas House
Quay Street
Manchester
M3 3HN

Tel: 0161 833 9244

Imperative, Bullying Helpline

Tel: 0181 885 1677 (Monday–Friday 7–9p.m.; Saturday 9.30–11.30a.m.)

Select bibliography

Books and booklets

Argyle, Michael (1988), *Bodily Communication*, London: Routledge.

Arroba, T. and James, K. (1987), *Pressure at Work: A Survival Guide*, London: McGraw-Hill.

Ashworth, Henry (1981), *Assertiveness at Work*, New York: McGraw-Hill.

Bibby, Pauline (1994), *Personal Safety for Social Workers*, Aldershot: Arena.

Bibby, Pauline (1995), *Personal Safety for Health Care Workers*, Aldershot: Arena.

Birmingham City Council Women's Unit (1989), *Facing Aggression at Work*, Birmingham City Council.

Breakwell, G. (1989), *Facing Physical Violence*, London: BPS Books/Routledge.

Cooper, Ken and Little, David (1996), *Managing Security in Schools and Colleges*, London: Secondary Heads Association, February.

Davies, Jessica (1990), *Protect Yourself*, London: Judy Piatkus.

Department of Education and Science (1987), *Building Bulletin 67: Crime Prevention in Schools*, London: DES.

Department for Education and Employment (1995), *Protecting Children from Abuse: The Role of the Education Service*, London: DfEE Publications.

Dickson, Anne (1986), *A Woman in Your Own Right: Assertiveness and You*, London: Quartet Books.

Education Service Advisory Committee (1990), *Violence to Staff in the Education Sector*, London: Health and Safety Executive.

Education Service Advisory Committee (1992), *The Responsibilities of School Governors for Health and Safety*, London: Health and Safety Executive.

Education Service Advisory Committee (1995), *Managing Health and Safety in Schools*, London: HMSO.

233

Egan, G. (1990), *The Skilled Helper*, London: Brooks/Cole.

Hanmer, J. and Saunders, S. (1984), *Well-founded Fear – A Community Study of Violence to Women*, London: Hutchinson.

Health and Safety Executive (1975), *Health and Safety at Work etc. Act: The Act Outlined*, London: HSE.

Health and Safety Executive (1988), *Preventing Violence to Staff*, London: HMSO.

Health and Safety Executive (1990), *A Guide to the Health and Safety at Work etc. Act 1974* (4th edn), London: HMSO.

Health and Safety Executive (1992), *Selecting a Health and Safety Consultancy*, London: HSE, IND (G) 133L.

Health and Safety Executive (1993), *Prevention of Violence to Staff in Banks and Building Societies*, London: HSE, HS (G) 100.

Health and Safety Executive (1994), *Safety Policies in the Education Sector* (rev. edn), London: HSE.

Hodge, Jeremy (1995), *Loss Prevention Council – Technical Briefing Note for Insurers – Violence At Work*, London: HSE.

Lamplugh, Diana (1988), *Beating Aggression – A Practical Guide for Working Women*, London: Weidenfeld and Nicolson.

Lamplugh, Diana (1991), *Without Fear – The Key to Staying Safe*, London: Weidenfeld and Nicolson.

Lamplugh, Diana (1994), *Violence and Aggression at Work: Reducing the Risks*, London: The Suzy Lamplugh Trust.

Lindenfield, Gael (1993), *Managing Anger*, London: Thorsons.

Library Association (1987), *Violence in Libraries*, London: Library Association.

North East Regionals Schools Security Group (1990), *Security in Schools: A Management Guide*, Newcastle upon Tyne: North East Regional Schools Security Group.

Phillips, C.M. and Stockdale, J.E. (1991), *Violence at Work – Issues, Policies and Procedures*, Luton: Local Government Management Board.

Suzy Lamplugh Trust (1989), *Reducing the Risk – Action Against Violence at Work*, London: The Suzy Lamplugh Trust.

Suzy Lamplugh Trust (1993), *A Guide to Safer Living*, London: The Suzy Lamplugh Trust.

Suzy Lamplugh Trust (1994), *Violence and Aggression at Work: Reducing the Risks – Guidance for Employers on Principles, Policy and Practice*, London: The Suzy Lamplugh Trust.

The Samaritans (1996), *Challenging the Taboo – Attitudes Towards Suicide and Depression*, London: The Samaritans.

West Midlands Police, in association with Sensormatic (1995), *Knowing Your School*, Birmingham: Sensormatic.

Articles

Adcock, J. (1988), 'Prevention of violence to staff', *Local Government Employment*, October.

Brockington, R. (1988), 'Violence to staff', *Local Government Employment*, August.

Castillo, D.N. and Jenkins, E.L. (1994), 'Industries and occupations at high risk for work-related homicide', *Journal of Occupational Medicine*, Vol. 36, No. 2, February.

Charter, David (1996), 'Girl bullies of the nineties "are moving from words to action" ', *The Times*, 2 May.

Cook, M. (1988), 'A rod for their own backs', *Education*, September.

Copeland, L. (1987), 'Travelling abroad safely: Some tips to give employees', *Personnel*, February.

Eaton, L. (1986), 'Lessons on tackling aggression', *Social Work Today*, December.

Eccles, K. and Tuff, N. (1987), 'Defence of the realm', *Insight*, December.

Francis, W. (1986), 'What the organisations say', *Community Care*, December.

Groombridge, B. (1989), 'Risky work', *Education*, May.

Hall, L. (1989), 'Attacking aggression', *Personnel Today*, May.

Health and Safety Executive (1988), 'Preventing violence to staff', *Health and Safety Information Bulletin*, No. 154, October.

Hill, C. (1989), 'Protecting employees from attack', *Personnel Management*, February.

Industrial Society Information Service (1989), 'Employers liable for violence to staff', *Industrial Society Magazine*, March.

Kelly, B. (1989) 'A case of wolves in sheep's clothing', *Local Government Chronicle*, April.

Lloyd, T. (1989), 'The problem with men', *Social Work Today*, September.

Moore, Wendy (1996), 'A violent occupation', The *Guardian*, 17 April.

Painter, K. (1987), 'It's part of the job', *Employee Relations*, Vol. 9, No. 5.

Passmore, J. (1989), 'Violent clients – service or safety?', *Housing Planning Review*, Vol. 44, No. 2, April/May.

Savery, L. and Gledhill, A. (1988), 'Sexual harassment of women in industry and commerce by co-workers: Some Australian evidence', *Personnel Review*, Vol. 17, No. 8.

Segal, L. (1989), 'The beast in man', *New Statesman and Society*, September.

Thomas, C. (1987), 'Staff security in housing offices', *Going Local*, No. 7, March, Bristol: SAUS (School for Advanced Urban Studies), Bristol University.

Tonkin, B. (1986), 'Quantifying risk factors', *Community Care*, November.

Whitehead, M. (1988), 'A violent war on the front line', *Local Government Employment*, February.

Williams, B. and Howe, A. (1988), 'Violence to staff – another possible answer', *Local Government Employment*, February.

Wills, J. (1987), 'Realising the risks', *Local Government Chronicle*, November.

Reports and papers

Balding, John, et al. (1996), *Cash and Carry*, Schools Health and Education Unit, Exeter University.

Consumers' Association (1990), 'Which? report on street crime', *Which?*, pp. 636–9.

Department for Education and Employment (1996), *School Security: Report of the Working Group*, London: DfEE.

Department for Education and Employment (1995), *Protecting Children From Abuse: The Role of the Education Service*, Circular 10/95, London: DfEE.

Department of Health and Social Security Advisory Committee on Violence to Staff (1988), *Violence to Staff*, London: HMSO.

Department of Transport (1986), *Assaults on Bus Staff and Measures to Prevent Such Assaults: Report of the Working Group on Violence to Road Passenger Transport Staff*, London: HMSO.

Elton Committee (1989), *Discipline in Schools: Report of the Committee of Inquiry Chaired by Lord Elton* (The Elton Report), London: HMSO.

Gulbenkian Foundation (1995), *Children and Violence*, London: Calouste Gulbenkian Foundation.

Health and Safety Executive (1992), *Management of Health and Safety Regulations 1992 – Approved Code of Practice*, London: HSE.

Health and Safety Executive (1996), *Reporting of Injuries, Diseases and Dangerous Occurrences Regulations*, London: HSE.

Home Office (1989), *Safer Cities – Progress Report 1989–1990*, London: Home Office Safer Cities Unit.

Home Office (1993), *Compensating Victims of Violent Crime: Changes to the Criminal Injuries Compensation Scheme*, Cm 2434, London: HMSO.

Home Office (1996), *Notifiable Offences – England and Wales 1995*, Statistical Bulletin 3/96, London: Government statistical Service.

Home Office Public Relations Branch (1984), *Fear of Crime in England and Wales: Report of the Working Group*, London: Home Office Public Relations Branch.

Home Office Research and Statistics Department (1988), *British Crime Survey*, London: HMSO.

Home Office Research and Statistics Department (1993), *British Crime Survey*, London: HMSO.

Home Office Standing Committee for Violence (1984), *Report of the Working*

Group – *Fear of Crime in England and Wales*, London: Home Office Public Relations Branch.

Income Data Services (1990), *Violence Against Staff*, Report No. 458, London: Income Data Services.

Income Data Services (1994), *Violence Against Staff*, Report No. 557, London: Income Data Services.

Labour Research Department (1987), *Assaults on Staff – Bargaining Report*, London: LRD, July.

Lamplugh, Diana (1996), *Personal Safety at Work, Special Issue: Gender and Life in Organisations*, Occasional Papers in Organisational Analysis, No. 5, Department of Business Management, University of Porstmouth.

Lewis, Edwin (1994), *Truancy – The Partnership Approach*, Stoke on Trent: Smith Davis Press.

Local Government Management Board (1991), *Violence at Work: Issues, Policies and Procedures – A Case Study of Two Local Authorities*, London: LGMB.

Manufacturing, Science and Finance Union (1993), *Prevention of Violence at Work*, MSF Health and Safety Information Bulletin No. 37, Bishop's Stortford: MSF.

Mayhew, P., Elliott, D. and Dowds, L. (1989), *The 1988 British Crime Survey*, Home Office Research Study No. 111, London: HMSO.

Mayhew, P., Aye Maung, N. and Mirrlees-Black, C. (1993), *The 1992 British Crime Survey*, Home Office Research Study No. 132, London: HMSO.

Mayhew, P., et al. (1994) *Research Findings No. 14 – Trends in Crime: Findings of the 1994 British Crime Survey*, London: Home Office Research and Statistics Department.

National Association of Head Teachers (1996), *Managing Risk Assessment*, Professional Management Series, Pamphlet No. PM008, London: NAHT, February.

National Union of Teachers (1996), *Security, Schools and the Community*, London: NUT.

Oxford Brookes University School of Planning (1994), *A Guide to Personal Safety for Young Travellers Abroad*, Oxford Brookes University.

Phillips, C.M., Stockdale, J.E. and Joeman, L.M. (1989), *The Risks in Going to Work*, London: The Suzy Lamplugh Trust.

Poyner, B. and Warne, C. (1986), *Violence to Staff – A Basis for Assessment and Prevention*, London: HMSO.

Poyner, B. and Warne, C. (1988), *Preventing Violence to Staff*, London: HMSO.

Rowett, C. (1986), *Violence in Social Work*, Occasional Paper No. 14, University of Cambridge, Institute of Criminology.

Stott, M. (1988), *Living Agenda: Report of a Conference at London University on Aggression and Vulnerability at Work*, London: The Suzy Lamplugh Trust.

Suzy Lamplugh Trust (1995), *Youth of Britain: Personal Safety Matters! Report of The Suzy Lamplugh Trust Conference 17 January 1995*, London: The Suzy Lamplugh Trust.

Trades Union Congress (1987), *Preventing Violence to Staff: Progress Report*, London: TUC.

Trades Union Congress (1988), *Violence to Staff: Progress Report*, London: TUC.

Training resources

Brook Street (1987), *Smart Moves*, St Albans: Brook Street.

Cardy, C. (1992), *Training for Personal Safety at Work*, Aldershot: Connaught Training.

Channel 4 Television (1988), *Assert Yourself*, London: Guild Training.

Leeds Animation Workshop (1983), *Give Us a Smile*, Leeds Animation Workshop.

Local Government Management Board (1987), *Dealing Effectively with Aggressive and Violent Customers*, Luton: LGMB.

Local Government Management Board (1987), *On the Front Line*, Luton: LGMB.

Metropolitan Police (1987), *Positive Steps*, London: Cygnet Films, in association with Norwich Union Insurance.

McGraw-Hill (1982), *Communicating Non-defensively – Don't Take it Personally*, McGraw-Hill Films.

Reynolds, N. (1982), *Personal Safety*, Rank Aldis.

Suzy Lamplugh Trust (1989), *Avoiding Danger*, London: Creative Vision.

Suzy Lamplugh Trust (1989), *You Can Cope: Lifeskills Training Pack*, Aldershot: Gower.

Suzy Lamplugh Trust (1991, 1994), *Well Safe* (secondary schools resource pack), London: The Suzy Lamplugh Trust.

Suzy Lamplugh Trust (1994), *Personal Safety at Work. Guidance for All Employees*, London: The Suzy Lamplugh Trust.

Suzy Lamplugh Trust (1995), *Well Safe for Teenagers* (video), London: The Suzy Lamplugh Trust.

Suzy Lamplugh Trust (1995), *On the Street? ... Well Get Streetwise* (pamphlet), London: The Suzy Lamplugh Trust.

Suzy Lamplugh Trust (1995), *Streetwise Poster for Teenagers*, London: Hascombe Enterprises.

Suzy Lamplugh Trust (1995), *Home Safe* (video, booklet, cards – personal safety for children), London: The Suzy Lamplugh Trust.

Suzy Lamplugh Trust (1996), *The Pocket Fast Guide to Personal Safety for People Who Work in Education*, London: Hascombe Enterprises.

Wiener, R. and Crosby, I. (1986), *Handling Violence and Aggression*, London: National Council for Voluntary Child Care.

Training available

Suzy Lamplugh Trust personal safety at work training is available throughout the UK. Please contact The Suzy Lamplugh Trust's training department for information:

14 East Sheen Avenue
London
SW14 8AS

Tel: 0181 876 0305.

Suzy Lamplugh Trust personal safety first course tutor courses, in association with London Central YMCA Training and Development, are also available throughout the UK. Please contact:

London Central YMCA
Training and Development
112 Great Russell Street
London
WC1B 3NQ

Tel: 0171 580 2989.

Useful organizations

ACAS
Head Office
Brandon House
180 Borough High Street
London
SE1 1LW

Tel: 0171 210 3000, or your local ACAS office.

Agency for Jewish Education
Woburn House
Upper Woburn Place
London
WC1H 0EP

Association of Metropolitan Authorities
35 Great Smith Street
London
SW1P 3BJ

Tel: 0171 222 8100

Association of Teachers and Lecturers
7 Northumberland Street
London
WC2N 5DA

Tel: 0171 930 6441

Belt Up School Kids (BUSK)
Head Office
Bwthyn Cadewn
Pen y Cae Mawr
Near Usk
NP5 1NA

Tel: 01291 672 488

British Association for Counselling
1 Regent Place
Rugby
Warwickshire
CV21 2PJ

Tel: 01788 550 899 (administration) 01788 578 328 (information)

Catholic Education Service
39 Eccleston Square
London
SW1V 1BX

Tel: 0171 828 7604

Church of England Board of Education
Church House
Great Smith Street
London
SW1P 3NZ

Tel: 0171 222 9011

Commission for Racial Equality
Elliot House
10–12 Allington Street
London
SW1E 5EH

Tel: 0171 828 7022

Crimestoppers Trust
100 West Hill
London
SW15 2UT

Tel: 0181 877 0337
Criminal Injuries Compensation Scheme
Morley House
26–30 Holborn Viaduct
London
EC1A 2JQ

Tel: 0171 842 6800

Department for Education and Employment
Sanctuary Buildings
Great Smith Street
London
SW1 3BT

Equal Opportunities Commission
Overseas House
Quay Street
Manchester
M3 3HN

Tel: 0171 222 1110 (press office) 0161 833 9244 (HQ Manchester)

Gender and Life in Organizations
Department of Business and Management
Portsmouth Business School
Locksway Road
Southsea
Hants
PO4 8JF

Tel: 01705 844 233 or 01705 844 060

Headmasters' and Headmistresses' Conference
130 Regent Road
Leicester
LE1 7PG

Tel: 0116 285 4810

Health and Safety Executive
Rose Court
2 Southwark Bridge
London
SE1 9HS

Tel: 0171 717 6000

Health and Safety Executive Books
PO Box 1999
Sudbury
Suffolk
CO10 6FS

Home Office
50 Queen Anne's Gate
London
SW1H 9AT

Safer Cities Unit – Department of the Environment
Tel: 0171 276 4505

Public Relations Branch
Tel: 0171 273 2193

Home Office Crime Prevention College
The Hawkhills
Easingwold
York
YO6 3EG

Tel: 01347 825 060

Imperative, Bullying Helpline

Tel: 0181 885 1677 (Monday–Friday 7–9p.m.; Saturday 9.30–11.30a.m.)

Industrial Society
48 Bryanston Square
London
W1H 7LN

Tel: 0171 262 2401

Kidscape
152 Buckingham Palace Road
London
SW1 9TR

Tel: 0171 730 3300

London Rape Crisis Centre
PO Box 69
London
WC1X 9NJ

Helpline: (6p.m.–10p.m. weekdays,
10a.m.–10p.m. weekends) 0171 837 1600

Tel: (office) 0171 916 5466

Minibus Driver Awareness Scheme
Community Transport Association
Highbank
Halton Street
Hyde
Cheshire
SK14 2NY

NASUWT
Hillscourt Education Centre
Rose Hill
Rednal
Birmingham
B45 8RS

Tel: 0121 453 6150

National Association of Head Teachers
1 Heath Square
Boltro Road
Haywards Heath
West Sussex
RH16 1BL

Tel: 0144 458 133

National Countering Bullying Unit
University of Wales Institute Cardiff
Cyn Coed Campus
Cyn Coed Road
Cardiff
CF2 6XD

Tel: 01222 506 781

National Governors Council
35 Hawthorn Road
Droylesden
Manchester
M43 7HU

National Union of Teachers
Hamilton House
Mabledon Place
London
WC1H 9BD

Tel: 0171 388 6191

Professional Association of Teachers
2 St James' Court
Friargate
Derby
DE 1BT

Tel: 01332 372 337

Secondary Heads' Association
130 Regent Road
Leicester
LE1 7PG

Tel: 0116 247 1797

Sensormatic
Harefield Grove
Rickmansworth Road
Harefield
Uxbridge
UB9 6JY

Tel: 0800 75 75 77

Suzy Lamplugh Trust
14 East Sheen Avenue
London
SW14 8AS

Tel: 0181 392 1839

Victim Support
Cranmer House
39 Brixton Road
Stockwell
London
SW9 5DZ

Tel: 0171 735 9166

The Suzy Lamplugh Trust
• personal safety resources for schools •

The Trust, the national charity for personal safety, is the only organization in the UK specializing in personal safety. The Trust has resources to help everyone, from the cradle to the grave, underpinned by expert tutors and trainers operating nationwide.

Training
of those who work in education

Personal Safety for Schools contains all the material necessary for a competent trainer to effect risk assessment as well as to design, plan and provide training to governors, managers, teachers and other staff.

However, some in-house trainers may feel they need extra knowledge and confidence in the teaching of personal safety. The Trust, with the YMCA Training and Development Unit, provides *Personal Safety First* training courses for such personnel.

The Trust can also provide talks, conferences, seminars and consultancy, or can arrange specially-designed courses with role plays and case studies, guided by Trust-registered trainers.

For further information contact:

Training & Resources Department
The Suzy Lamplugh Trust
14 East Sheen Avenue
London SW14 8AS
Tel: 0181 876 0305

The Pocket Fast Guide to Personal Safety for People Who Work in Education is an aide-mémoire of *Personal Safety for Schools* and an essential pocket guide for every employee. It suggests some of the skills and strategies that individuals can develop to improve personal safety: assessing and reducing the risks, dealing with aggression, what to do if attacked, and how to cope while travelling and away from home.

Available from The Trust • Price: £5.29 – Discounts for bulk orders